CONSUMER PRICE INDEX – JANUARY 2015

The Consumer Price Index for All Urban Consumers (CPI-U) declined 0.7 percent in January on a seasonally adjusted basis, the U.S. Bureau of Labor Statistics reported today. Over the last 12 months, the all items index decreased 0.1 percent before seasonal adjustment.

The energy index fell 9.7 percent as the gasoline index fell 18.7 percent in January, the sharpest in a series of seven consecutive declines. The gasoline decrease was overwhelmingly the cause of the decline in the all items index, which would have risen 0.1 percent had the gasoline index been unchanged. The fuel oil index also fell sharply, and the index for natural gas turned down, although the electricity index rose. The food index was unchanged in January, with the food at home index falling for the first time since May 2013.

The index for all items less food and energy rose 0.2 percent in January. The shelter index rose 0.3 percent, and the indexes for personal care, for apparel, and for recreation increased as well. The medical care index was unchanged, while an array of indexes declined in January, including those for household furnishings and operations, alcoholic beverages, new vehicles, used cars and trucks, airline fares, and tobacco.

The all items index declined 0.1 percent over the last 12 months, the first negative 12-month change since the period ending October 2009. The energy index fell 19.6 percent over the span, with the gasoline index down 35.4 percent. The food index rose 3.2 percent, and the index for all items less food and energy increased 1.6 percent.

Chart 1. One-month percent change in CPI for All Urban Consumers (CPI-U), seasonally adjusted, Jan. 2014 - Jan. 2015
Percent change

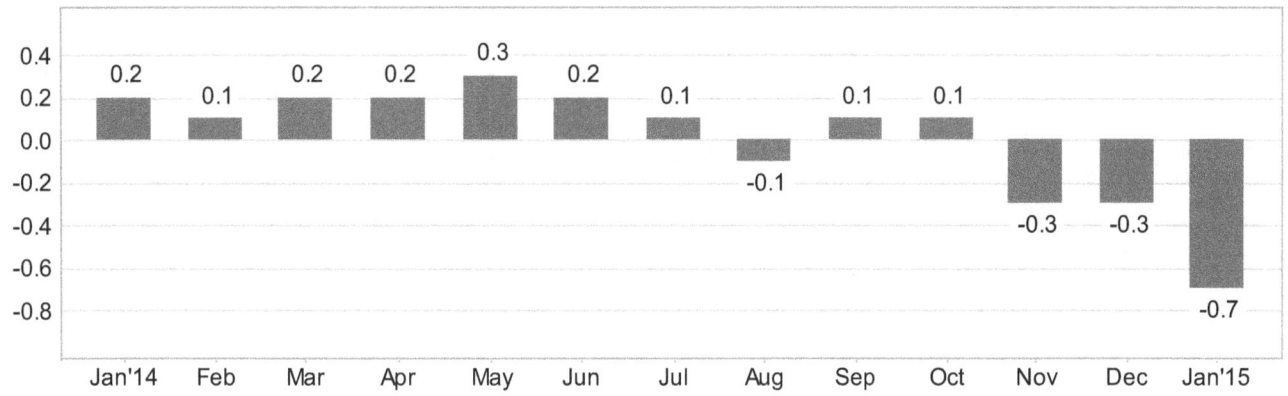

Chart 2. 12-month percent change in CPI for All Urban Consumers (CPI-U), not seasonally adjusted, Jan. 2014 - Jan. 2015
Percent change

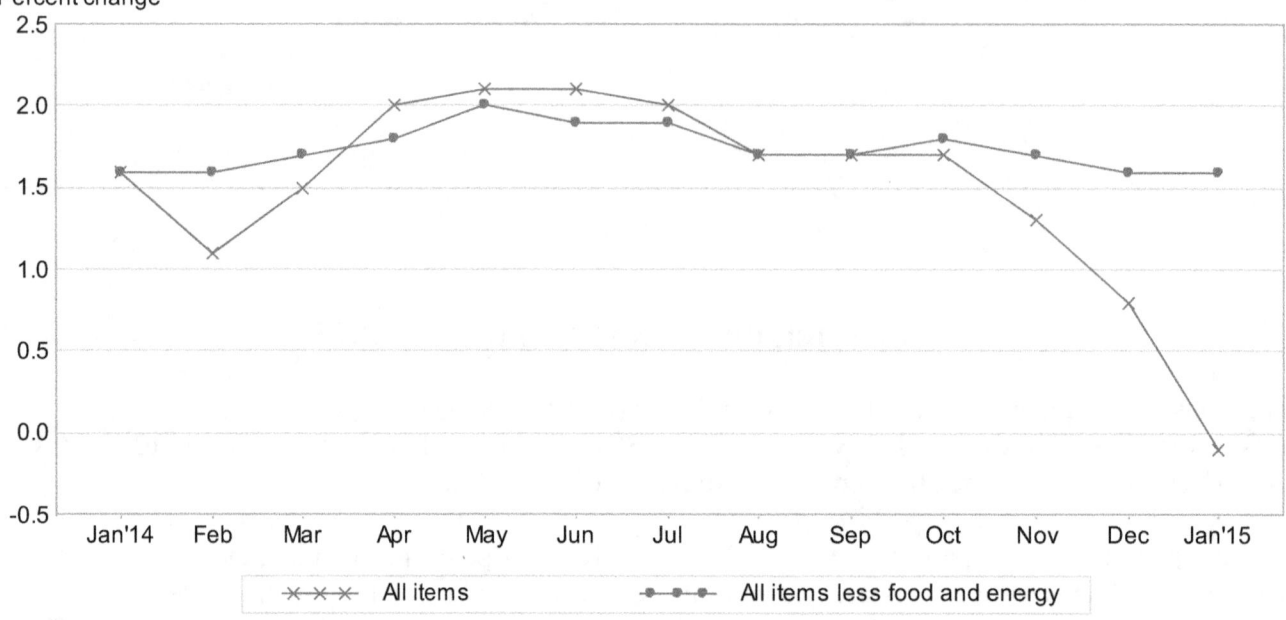

Table A. Percent changes in CPI for All Urban Consumers (CPI-U): U.S. city average

	Seasonally adjusted changes from preceding month							Un-adjusted 12-mos. ended Jan. 2015
	July 2014	Aug. 2014	Sep. 2014	Oct. 2014	Nov. 2014	Dec. 2014	Jan. 2015	
All items	.1	-.1	.1	.1	-.3	-.3	-.7	-.1
Food	.3	.3	.3	.2	.2	.2	.0	3.2
Food at home	.3	.3	.3	.2	.1	.2	-.2	3.3
Food away from home [1]	.3	.2	.3	.2	.4	.3	.2	3.1
Energy	-.2	-1.7	-.7	-1.2	-4.1	-4.7	-9.7	-19.6
Energy commodities	-.4	-2.6	-.9	-2.1	-7.0	-9.0	-18.0	-34.7
Gasoline (all types)	-.4	-2.7	-.9	-2.0	-7.2	-9.2	-18.7	-35.4
Fuel oil [1]	-.7	-1.2	-2.1	-4.0	-3.5	-7.8	-9.9	-29.7
Energy services	.2	-.3	-.4	-.1	-.3	.8	-.1	1.9
Electricity	.2	.2	-.7	.5	.0	.6	.9	2.5
Utility (piped) gas service ...	.0	-1.9	.4	-1.9	-1.3	1.4	-3.4	-.4
All items less food and energy	.1	.1	.1	.2	.1	.1	.2	1.6
Commodities less food and energy commodities	.0	-.1	.1	.0	-.3	-.2	-.1	-.8
New vehicles	.3	.1	.0	.1	.0	.0	-.1	.5
Used cars and trucks	-.1	.0	.0	-.6	-.9	-.8	-.1	-4.0
Apparel	.1	-.4	.1	-.3	-.7	-.8	.3	-1.4
Medical care commodities ...	.3	.0	.5	.2	.6	.9	-.3	3.9
Services less energy services	.1	.1	.2	.2	.2	.2	.3	2.5
Shelter	.3	.2	.3	.2	.2	.2	.3	2.9
Transportation services	-.6	-.3	.1	.5	.2	.0	.4	2.1
Medical care services	.1	.1	.1	.2	.3	.3	.1	2.3

[1] Not seasonally adjusted.

Consumer Price Index Data for January 2015

Food

The food index was unchanged in January after rising through all of 2014. The index for food at home turned down in January, falling 0.2 percent after increasing in each of the last 6 months. Four of the six major grocery store food groups declined in January. The fruits and vegetables index fell 0.9 percent, with the indexes for fresh fruits and fresh vegetables both declining. The dairy and related products index also fell 0.9 percent, its largest decline since April 2012. The index for meats, poultry, fish, and eggs fell slightly in January, decreasing 0.1 percent despite the index for beef and veal rising 0.1 percent. The index for other food at home, which rose in November and December, also declined 0.1 percent in January. The food at home index has increased 3.3 percent over the last 12 months, with all six major grocery store food group indexes rising over that span. The largest increase was posted by the meats, poultry, fish, and eggs group, which rose 8.7 percent with the beef and veal index increasing 19.0 percent. The index for food away from home increased 0.2 percent in January after a 0.3-percent increase in December and has risen 3.1 percent over the last 12 months.

Energy

The energy index fell 9.7 percent in January, its seventh consecutive decline and the largest 1-month decrease since November 2008. The 18.7-percent decline in the gasoline index was the main factor. (Before seasonal adjustment, gasoline prices fell 17.1 percent in January.) The fuel oil index also fell sharply, declining 9.9 percent after a 7.8-percent decline in December. The index for natural gas, which rose in December, fell 3.4 percent in January. The electricity index was the only major energy component to increase, rising 0.9 percent, its largest increase since May 2014. The electricity index is also the only major energy component to rise over the last 12 months, increasing 2.5 percent over the span. The gasoline and fuel oil indexes have declined sharply over the period, falling 35.4 percent and 29.7 percent, respectively. The index for natural gas has declined slightly over the span, decreasing 0.4 percent.

All items less food and energy

The index for all items less food and energy increased 0.2 percent in January. The shelter index increased 0.3 percent, with the rent and owners' equivalent rent indexes both rising 0.2 percent and the index for lodging away from home rising 1.3 percent. The personal care index rose 0.6 percent in January, its largest increase since the inception of the index in 1999. The apparel index rose 0.3 percent, and the recreation index increased 0.2 percent. The index for medical care was unchanged in January, with the index for medical care services rising, but the medical care commodities index falling. Several indexes posted modest declines in January. The index for household furnishings and operations fell 0.2 percent, and the indexes for new vehicles and for used cars and trucks both fell 0.1 percent. The index for alcoholic beverages fell 0.3 percent, as did the index for airline fares. The tobacco index also declined, falling 0.2 percent after rising in December.

The index for all items less food and energy has risen 1.6 percent over the past 12 months, the same figure as for the 12 months ending December. The index for shelter has risen 2.9 percent over the span, and the indexes for medical care, for new vehicles, and for alcoholic beverages are among those that have also increased. Indexes that have declined over the past year include those for used cars and trucks, airline fares, household furnishings and operations, and apparel.

Not seasonally adjusted CPI measures

The Consumer Price Index for All Urban Consumers (CPI-U) decreased 0.1 percent over the last 12 months to an index level of 233.707 (1982-84=100). For the month, the index fell 0.5 percent prior to seasonal adjustment.

The Consumer Price Index for Urban Wage Earners and Clerical Workers (CPI-W) decreased 0.8 percent over the last 12 months to an index level of 228.294 (1982-84=100). For the month, the index fell 0.7 percent prior to seasonal adjustment.

The Chained Consumer Price Index for All Urban Consumers (C-CPI-U) decreased 0.6 percent over the last 12 months. For the month, the index fell 0.7 percent on a not seasonally adjusted basis. Please note that the indexes for the past 10 to 12 months are subject to revision.

———————————

The Consumer Price Index for February 2015 is scheduled to be released on Tuesday, March 24, 2015, at 8:30 a.m. (EDT).

Chained Consumer Price Index to be Revised Quarterly

Effective with this release of CPI data for January 2015 on February 26, 2015, the Bureau of Labor Statistics is beginning quarterly revisions of the Chained Consumer Price Index for All Urban Consumers (C-CPI-U). In addition, a Constant Elasticity of Substitution (CES) formula will replace the geometric mean formula for the calculation of Initial and Interim C-CPI-U indexes.

More frequent weight updates and index revisions. Whereas CPI-U and CPI-W indexes are considered final when released, the final C-CPI-U index is published with a lag for administration and processing of Consumer Expenditure Survey household data, the source of the final C-CPI-U monthly expenditure weights. Under the traditional annual revision process, the final C-CPI-U index was published 13 to 24 months after the CPI-U. The CPI program is implementing a new estimation system that calculates monthly expenditure weights and revised C-CPI-U indexes on a quarterly basis. Under the new quarterly process, the final C-CPI-U index will lag the CPI-U index by 10 to 12 months.

Final C-CPI-U indexes for 2014 will be published on the following quarterly schedule:

Index Month	Release Month
January 2013 – March 2014	February 2015
April – June 2014	May 2015
July – September 2014	August 2015
October – December 2014	November 2015

Initial C-CPI-U indexes will continue to be released concurrent with the CPI-U release, and will be updated as interim C-CPI-U indexes with every quarterly revision until the final version is published.

New formula for initial and interim C-CPI-U Indexes. The CES formula will replace the geometric mean formula for initial and interim C-CPI-U indexes effective with this February 26, 2015 release. The CES formula is an improvement over the geometric mean formula because the CES formula more closely models consumer substitution behavior.

With the use of the geometric mean formula, consumers are assumed to consistently substitute within item classification to goods whose prices are falling relative to others. Using a fixed quantity formula, such as a Laspeyres formula, consumers are assumed to make no substitutions between goods when faced with relative price change. In reality, consumers respond to relative price changes differently than either model implies. The CES formula attempts to capture the amount of substitution occurring in the marketplace as consumers respond to changing relative prices.

For further details on the implementation of the CES formula and the frequency of weight updates for the C-CPI-U, please contact the CPI Information and Analysis section at (202) 691-6966.

New Estimation System

Effective with this release of the January 2015 CPI on February 26, 2015, the Bureau of Labor Statistics is utilizing a new estimation system for the Consumer Price Index. The new estimation system, the first major improvement to the existing system in over 25 years, is a redesigned, state-of-the-art system with improved flexibility and review capabilities. For more information on this new system, please see http://www.bls.gov/cpi/cpinewest.htm.

Facilities for Sensory Impaired

Information from this release will be made available to sensory impaired individuals upon request. Voice phone: 202-691-5200, Federal Relay Services: 1-800-877-8339.

Brief Explanation of the CPI

The Consumer Price Index (CPI) is a measure of the average change in prices over time of goods and services purchased by households. The Bureau of Labor Statistics publishes CPIs for two population groups: (1) the CPI for Urban Wage Earners and Clerical Workers (CPI-W), which covers households of wage earners and clerical workers that comprise approximately 28 percent of the total population and (2) the CPI for All Urban Consumers (CPI-U) and the Chained CPI for All Urban Consumers (C-CPI-U), which covers approximately 89 percent of the total population and includes, in addition to wage earners and clerical worker households, groups such as professional, managerial, and technical workers, the self-employed, short-term workers, the unemployed, and retirees and others not in the labor force.

The CPIs are based on prices of food, clothing, shelter, and fuels, transportation fares, charges for doctors' and dentists' services, drugs, and other goods and services that people buy for day-to-day living. Prices are collected each month in 87 urban areas across the country from about 4,000 housing units and approximately 26,000 retail establishments-department stores, supermarkets, hospitals, filling stations, and other types of stores and service establishments. All taxes directly associated with the purchase and use of items are included in the index. Prices of fuels and a few other items are obtained every month in all 87 locations. Prices of most other commodities and services are collected every month in the three largest geographic areas and every other month in other areas. Prices of most goods and services are obtained by personal visits or telephone calls of the Bureau's trained representatives.

In calculating the index, price changes for the various items in each location are averaged together with weights, which represent their importance in the spending of the appropriate population group. Local data are then combined to obtain a U.S. city average. For the CPI-U and CPI-W separate indexes are also published by size of city, by region of the country, for cross-classifications of regions and population-size classes, and for 27 local areas. Area indexes do not measure differences in the level of prices among cities; they only measure the average change in prices for each area since the base period. For the C-CPI-U data are issued only at the national level. It is important to note that the CPI-U and CPI-W are considered final when released, but the C-CPI-U is issued in preliminary form and subject to two annual revisions.

The index measures price change from a designed reference date. For the CPI-U and the CPI-W the reference base is 1982-84 equals 100. The reference base for the C-CPI-U is December 1999 equals 100. An increase of 16.5 percent from the reference base, for example, is shown as 116.500. This change can also be expressed in dollars as follows: the price of a base period market basket of goods and services in the CPI has risen from $10 in 1982-84 to $11.65.

For further details visit the CPI home page on the Internet at http://www.bls.gov/cpi/ or contact our CPI Information and Analysis Section on (202) 691-7000.

Note on Sampling Error in the Consumer Price Index

The CPI is a statistical estimate that is subject to sampling error because it is based upon a sample of retail prices and not the complete universe of all prices. BLS calculates and publishes estimates of the 1-month, 2-month, 6-month and 12-month percent change standard errors annually, for the CPI-U. These standard error estimates can be used to construct confidence intervals for hypothesis testing. For example, the estimated standard error of the 1 month percent change is 0.04 percent for the U.S. All Items Consumer Price Index. This means that if we repeatedly sample from the universe of all retail prices using the same methodology, and estimate a percentage change for each sample, then 95% of these estimates would be within 0.08 percent of the 1 month percentage change based on all retail prices. For example, for a 1-month change of 0.2 percent in the All Items CPI for All Urban Consumers, we are 95 percent confident that the actual percent change based on all retail prices would fall between 0.12 and 0.28 percent. For the latest data, including information on how to use the estimates of standard error, see "Variance Estimates for Price Changes in the Consumer Price Index, January-December 2013". These data are available on the CPI home page (http://www.bls.gov/cpi), or by using the following link: http://www.bls.gov/cpi/cpivar2013.pdf

Calculating Index Changes

Movements of the indexes from one month to another are usually expressed as percent changes rather than changes in index points, because index point changes are affected by the level of the index in relation to its base period while percent changes are not. The example below illustrates the computation of index point and percent changes.

Percent changes for 3-month and 6-month periods are expressed as annual rates and are computed according to the standard formula for compound growth rates. These data indicate what the percent change would be if the current rate were maintained for a 12-month period.

Index Point Change

CPI	202.416
Less previous index	201.800
Equals index point change	.616

Percent Change

Index point difference	.616
Divided by the previous index	201.800
Equals	0.003
Results multiplied by one hundred	0.003x100
Equals percent change	0.3

A Note on Seasonally Adjusted and Unadjusted Data

Because price data are used for different purposes by different groups, the Bureau of Labor Statistics publishes seasonally adjusted as well as unadjusted changes each month.

For analyzing general price trends in the economy, seasonally adjusted changes are usually preferred since they eliminate the effect of changes that normally occur at the same time and in about the same magnitude every year--such as price movements resulting from changing climatic conditions, production cycles, model changeovers, holidays, and sales.

The unadjusted data are of primary interest to consumers concerned about the prices they actually pay. Unadjusted data also are used extensively for escalation purposes. Many collective bargaining contract agreements and pension plans, for example, tie compensation changes to the Consumer Price Index before adjustment for seasonal variation.

Seasonal factors used in computing the seasonally adjusted indexes are derived by the X-13ARIMA-SEATS Seasonal Adjustment Method. Seasonally adjusted indexes and seasonal factors are computed annually. Each year, the last five years of seasonally adjusted data are revised. Data from January 2010 through December 2014 were replaced in January 2015. Exceptions to the usual revision schedule were: the updated seasonal data at the end of 1977 replaced data from 1967 through 1977; and, in January 2002, dependently seasonally adjusted series were revised for January 1987-December 2001 as a result of a change in the aggregation weights for dependently adjusted series. For further information, please see "Aggregation of Dependently Adjusted Seasonally Adjusted Series," in the October 2001 issue of the CPI Detailed Report.

Effective with the publication of data from January 2006 through December 2010 in January 2011, the Video and audio series and the Information technology, hardware and services series were changed from independently adjusted to dependently adjusted. This resulted in an increase in the number of seasonal components used in deriving seasonal movement of the All items and 64 other lower level aggregations, from 73 for the publication of January 1998 through December 2005 data to 82 for the publication of seasonally adjusted data for January 2006 and later. Each year the seasonal status of every series is reevaluated based upon certain statistical criteria. If any of the 82 components change their seasonal adjustment status from seasonally adjusted to not seasonally adjusted, not seasonally adjusted data will be used in the aggregation of the dependent series for the last five years, but the seasonally adjusted indexes before that period will not be changed. Note: 32 of the 82 components are not seasonally adjusted for 2014.

Seasonally adjusted data, including the all items index levels, are subject to revision for up to five years after their original release. For this reason, BLS advises against the use of these data in escalation agreements.

Effective with the calculation of the seasonal factors for 1990, the Bureau of Labor Statistics has used an enhanced seasonal adjustment procedure called Intervention Analysis Seasonal Adjustment for some CPI series. Intervention Analysis Seasonal Adjustment allows for better estimates of seasonally adjusted data. Extreme values and/or sharp movements which might distort the seasonal pattern are estimated and removed from the data prior to calculation of seasonal factors. Beginning with the calculation of seasonal factors for 1996, X-12-ARIMA software was used for Intervention Analysis Seasonal Adjustment. In 2014, for the 2009-2013 revisions, the Bureau of Labor Statistics began using

X-13ARIMA-SEATS to perform the seasonal adjustment of CPI series, including Intervention Analysis Seasonal Adjustment for certain series.

For the seasonal factors introduced in January 2015, BLS adjusted 33 series using Intervention Analysis Seasonal Adjustment, including selected food and beverage items, motor fuels, electricity and vehicles. For example, this procedure was used for the Motor fuel series to offset the effects of events such as the response in crude oil markets to the worldwide economic downturn in 2008.

For a complete list of Intervention Analysis Seasonal Adjustment series and explanations, please refer to the article "Intervention Analysis Seasonal Adjustment", located on our website at http://www.bls.gov/cpi/cpisapage.htm.

For additional information on seasonal adjustment in the CPI, please write to the Bureau of Labor Statistics, Division of Consumer Prices and Price Indexes, Washington, DC 20212 or contact Chris Graci at (202) 691-5826, or by e-mail at graci.christopher@bls.gov or contact Carlyle Jackson at (202) 691-6984, or by e-mail at jackson.carlyle@bls.gov . If you have general questions about the CPI, please call our information staff at (202) 691-7000.

Revised seasonally adjusted changes

Over-the-month percent changes in the U.S. City Average Consumer Price Index for All Urban Consumers (CPI-U) for All Items and for All Items less food and energy, seasonally adjusted, using former and recalculated seasonal factors for 2014.

All Items

2014	Former	Recalculated	Difference
January	.1	.2	.1
February	.1	.1	.0
March	.2	.2	.0
April	.3	.2	-.1
May	.4	.3	-.1
June	.3	.2	-.1
July	.1	.1	.0
August	-.2	-.1	.1
September	.1	.1	.0
October	.0	.1	.1
November	-.3	-.3	.0
December	-.4	-.3	.1

All Items less food and energy

2014	Former	Recalculated	Difference
January	.1	.1	.0
February	.1	.1	.0
March	.2	.2	.0
April	.2	.2	.0
May	.3	.2	-.1
June	.1	.1	.0
July	.1	.1	.0
August	.0	.1	.1
September	.1	.1	.0
October	.2	.2	.0
November	.1	.1	.0
December	.0	.1	.1

Table 1. Consumer Price Index for All Urban Consumers (CPI-U): U.S. city average, by expenditure category, January 2015

[1982-84=100, unless otherwise noted]

Expenditure category	Relative importance Dec. 2014	Unadjusted indexes			Unadjusted percent change		Seasonally adjusted percent change		
		Jan. 2014	Dec. 2014	Jan. 2015	Jan. 2014-Jan. 2015	Dec. 2014-Jan. 2015	Oct. 2014-Nov. 2014	Nov. 2014-Dec. 2014	Dec. 2014-Jan. 2015
All items...	100.000	233.916	234.812	233.707	-0.1	-0.5	-0.3	-0.3	-0.7
Food...	14.257	238.872	245.976	246.538	3.2	0.2	0.2	0.2	0.0
Food at home..................................	8.427	235.356	242.457	243.123	3.3	0.3	0.1	0.2	-0.2
Cereals and bakery products...........	1.138	271.151	270.635	273.589	0.9	1.1	-0.1	0.2	0.7
Meats, poultry, fish, and eggs...........	2.014	240.158	261.055	260.982	8.7	0.0	0.7	0.4	-0.1
Dairy and related products[1].............	0.898	219.362	229.870	227.800	3.8	-0.9	-0.2	0.6	-0.9
Fruits and vegetables....................	1.379	292.095	297.429	298.781	2.3	0.5	-0.7	0.3	-0.9
Nonalcoholic beverages and beverage materials.................................	0.955	167.039	166.978	168.603	0.9	1.0	0.5	-0.4	0.1
Other food at home.......................	2.043	204.575	206.831	207.218	1.3	0.2	0.2	0.2	-0.1
Food away from home[1].....................	5.830	245.481	252.628	253.037	3.1	0.2	0.4	0.3	0.2
Energy...	8.030	239.551	209.785	192.619	-19.6	-8.2	-4.1	-4.7	-9.7
Energy commodities.........................	4.215	294.165	230.195	192.221	-34.7	-16.5	-7.0	-9.0	-18.0
Fuel oil[1].....................................	0.139	389.522	303.844	273.718	-29.7	-9.9	-3.5	-7.8	-9.9
Motor fuel....................................	3.979	288.268	225.165	186.763	-35.2	-17.1	-7.2	-9.2	-18.6
Gasoline (all types).....................	3.904	286.607	223.404	185.142	-35.4	-17.1	-7.2	-9.2	-18.7
Energy services[2]...........................	3.815	197.919	199.592	201.594	1.9	1.0	-0.3	0.8	-0.1
Electricity[2].................................	2.940	203.026	204.275	208.172	2.5	1.9	0.0	0.6	0.9
Utility (piped) gas service[2]...............	0.875	179.982	182.908	179.184	-0.4	-2.0	-1.3	1.4	-3.4
All items less food and energy...............	77.713	235.367	238.775	239.248	1.6	0.2	0.1	0.1	0.2
Commodities less food and energy commodities.............................	19.408	146.025	145.127	144.865	-0.8	-0.2	-0.3	-0.2	-0.1
Apparel.......................................	3.343	124.275	123.942	122.527	-1.4	-1.1	-0.7	-0.8	0.3
New vehicles...............................	3.551	145.880	146.524	146.558	0.5	0.0	0.0	0.0	-0.1
Used cars and trucks....................	1.591	147.386	141.957	141.461	-4.0	-0.3	-0.9	-0.8	-0.1
Medical care commodities...............	1.772	336.756	349.750	349.980	3.9	0.1	0.6	0.9	-0.3
Alcoholic beverages.....................	1.015	236.340	238.856	238.718	1.0	-0.1	0.6	-0.3	-0.3
Tobacco and smoking products.........	0.718	896.539	916.707	917.733	2.4	0.1	0.3	0.4	-0.2
Services less energy services.............	58.305	289.779	296.021	296.979	2.5	0.3	0.2	0.2	0.3
Shelter...................................	32.711	266.754	273.598	274.589	2.9	0.4	0.2	0.2	0.3
Rent of primary residence[2]...........	7.159	272.317	280.874	281.572	3.4	0.2	0.3	0.2	0.2
Owners' equivalent rent of residences[2, 3].........................	24.339	274.740	281.288	281.980	2.6	0.2	0.2	0.2	0.2
Medical care services....................	5.944	459.618	468.393	470.030	2.3	0.3	0.3	0.3	0.1
Physicians' services[2]..................	1.590	356.796	361.659	362.740	1.7	0.3	0.4	0.2	0.1
Hospital services[2, 4].....................	1.853	272.485	282.547	284.225	4.3	0.6	0.3	0.5	0.2
Transportation services..................	5.625	280.687	286.585	286.644	2.1	0.0	0.2	0.0	0.4
Motor vehicle maintenance and repair[1]...................................	1.168	263.718	268.588	268.869	2.0	0.1	0.1	0.1	0.1
Motor vehicle insurance................	2.300	429.585	448.933	451.007	5.0	0.5	0.3	0.3	0.6
Airline fare.................................	0.702	291.836	287.175	283.152	-3.0	-1.4	-0.2	-2.0	-0.3

[1] Not seasonally adjusted.

[2] This index series was calculated using a Laspeyres estimator. All other item stratum index series were calculated using a geometric means estimator.

[3] Indexes on a December 1982=100 base.

[4] Indexes on a December 1996=100 base.

NOTE: Index applies to a month as a whole, not to any specific date.

Table 2. Consumer Price Index for All Urban Consumers (CPI-U): U.S. city average, by detailed expenditure category, January 2015

[1982-84=100, unless otherwise noted]

Expenditure category	Relative importance Dec. 2014	Unadjusted percent change		Seasonally adjusted percent change		
		Jan. 2014- Jan. 2015	Dec. 2014- Jan. 2015	Oct. 2014- Nov. 2014	Nov. 2014- Dec. 2014	Dec. 2014- Jan. 2015
All items...	100.000	-0.1	-0.5	-0.3	-0.3	-0.7
Food..	14.257	3.2	0.2	0.2	0.2	0.0
Food at home.......................................	8.427	3.3	0.3	0.1	0.2	-0.2
Cereals and bakery products....................	1.138	0.9	1.1	-0.1	0.2	0.7
Cereals and cereal products....................	0.370	0.2	1.7	-0.5	-0.2	1.2
Flour and prepared flour mixes................	0.048	0.1	6.4	0.1	-1.1	2.1
Breakfast cereal[1]...............................	0.197	0.0	-0.6	0.7	-0.1	-0.6
Rice, pasta, cornmeal[1]........................	0.126	0.6	3.4	-1.7	-1.1	3.4
Rice[1, 2, 3]...		-1.4	1.1	-1.1	-1.0	1.1
Bakery products.................................	0.767	1.2	0.8	0.2	0.4	0.4
Bread[2]..	0.230	1.0	-0.4	0.2	0.8	-0.2
White bread[1, 3].............................		0.2	0.2	-0.2	1.4	0.2
Bread other than white[1, 3]................		1.2	-1.0	0.2	1.6	-1.0
Fresh biscuits, rolls, muffins[1, 2].............	0.116	3.1	1.2	0.5	0.2	1.1
Cakes, cupcakes, and cookies................	0.189	1.8	0.7	0.0	0.3	1.3
Cookies[1, 3]....................................		1.6	0.8	0.1	-0.1	1.5
Fresh cakes and cupcakes[1, 3]............		1.9	0.7	-0.7	0.1	0.7
Other bakery products..........................	0.233	0.1	1.9	0.2	0.0	0.2
Fresh sweetrolls, coffeecakes, doughnuts[1, 3]....		-0.6	0.6	-0.5	1.8	0.6
Crackers, bread, and cracker products[3].........		-0.2	1.7	0.3	-0.1	-0.4
Frozen and refrigerated bakery products, pies, tarts, turnovers[3]....................		0.6	2.4	1.0	-0.7	0.2
Meats, poultry, fish, and eggs..................	2.014	8.7	0.0	0.7	0.4	-0.1
Meats, poultry, and fish.........................	1.880	8.7	0.2	0.6	0.1	0.1
Meats..	1.229	12.6	0.1	0.5	0.4	0.1
Beef and veal[1].................................	0.582	19.0	0.1	0.8	0.7	0.1
Uncooked ground beef[1].....................	0.238	21.0	1.3	1.4	0.2	1.3
Uncooked beef roasts[1, 2]...................	0.085	21.6	-1.1	2.0	1.4	-1.1
Uncooked beef steaks[1, 2]..................	0.207	14.9	-0.7	-0.9	0.9	-0.7
Uncooked other beef and veal[1, 2].........	0.053	22.5	-0.2	2.7	1.2	-0.2
Pork..	0.372	7.4	-0.1	0.1	-0.2	-0.4
Bacon, breakfast sausage, and related products[2].....................	0.141	2.3	1.2	-0.1	-0.1	0.3
Bacon and related products[3]..............		-0.1	0.3	-0.5	-0.2	0.0
Breakfast sausage and related products[2, 3]...		6.2	2.4	0.5	0.4	0.6
Ham..	0.078	11.5	-0.5	1.2	-0.4	-1.0
Ham, excluding canned[3].....................		12.3	-0.9	1.3	-0.8	-1.3
Pork chops..	0.064	8.2	-2.0	-0.6	0.2	-2.0
Other pork including roasts and picnics[2].........	0.089	12.3	-0.5	-0.8	-0.6	-0.5
Other meats......................................	0.275	7.3	0.2	0.5	0.5	0.7
Frankfurters[3]....................................		10.3	-0.5	1.3	3.5	0.3
Lunchmeats[2, 3].................................		6.6	0.6	0.3	0.0	1.4
Lamb and organ meats[1, 3]...................		8.0	-0.5	1.6	-0.5	-0.5
Lamb and mutton[1, 2, 3].......................		3.2	0.6	1.4	-1.1	0.6
Poultry...	0.360	2.0	0.7	1.4	-0.4	0.5
Chicken[1, 2].......................................	0.294	2.9	0.4	1.2	-0.3	0.4
Fresh whole chicken[1, 3]......................		6.1	1.9	0.7	0.5	1.9
Fresh and frozen chicken parts[1, 3].........		1.4	-0.4	1.6	-0.5	-0.4
Other poultry including turkey[2]..................	0.066	-1.7	1.9	1.4	-1.4	-0.8
Fish and seafood[1]..............................	0.291	2.2	0.2	0.1	-0.3	-0.5
Fresh fish and seafood[2].......................	0.148	3.5	0.8	0.1	-0.1	0.0
Processed fish and seafood[2]..................	0.142	0.9	-0.5	0.4	-0.7	-0.8
Shelf stable fish and seafood[1, 3]............		0.2	-0.3	0.9	-1.0	-0.3

See footnotes at end of table.

Table 2. Consumer Price Index for All Urban Consumers (CPI-U): U.S. city average, by detailed expenditure category, January 2015 — Continued

[1982-84=100, unless otherwise noted]

Expenditure category	Relative importance Dec. 2014	Unadjusted percent change		Seasonally adjusted percent change		
		Jan. 2014-Jan. 2015	Dec. 2014-Jan. 2015	Oct. 2014-Nov. 2014	Nov. 2014-Dec. 2014	Dec. 2014-Jan. 2015
Frozen fish and seafood[3]		2.3	-0.5	0.5	-0.3	-1.0
Eggs	0.134	8.2	-3.3	1.1	4.1	-1.8
Dairy and related products[1]	0.898	3.8	-0.9	-0.2	0.6	-0.9
Milk[1, 2]	0.283	1.1	-2.2	-0.4	0.8	-2.2
Fresh whole milk[1, 3]		2.1	-1.5	0.1	-0.1	-1.5
Fresh milk other than whole[1, 2, 3]		0.7	-2.5	-0.6	1.5	-2.5
Cheese and related products	0.286	7.8	-0.5	0.3	0.2	-1.5
Ice cream and related products	0.126	2.0	-0.2	0.2	2.0	-1.3
Other dairy and related products[1, 2]	0.204	3.4	-0.1	-0.4	0.5	-0.1
Fruits and vegetables	1.379	2.3	0.5	-0.7	0.3	-0.9
Fresh fruits and vegetables	1.076	2.9	0.1	-0.8	0.3	-1.1
Fresh fruits	0.575	1.7	-0.9	-2.6	-1.1	-0.9
Apples	0.083	0.6	2.6	-0.6	-1.1	1.2
Bananas	0.087	-1.3	-0.2	1.5	-1.8	-1.2
Citrus fruits[2]	0.146	2.9	-1.6	-0.9	-0.9	-0.9
Oranges, including tangerines[3]		2.9	-0.4	0.5	-0.9	1.0
Other fresh fruits[2]	0.259	2.4	-1.8	-3.1	0.5	-2.0
Fresh vegetables	0.500	4.3	1.2	1.4	1.9	-1.4
Potatoes	0.075	-0.9	6.8	-1.3	1.0	1.5
Lettuce	0.072	12.2	5.3	2.6	-2.8	5.0
Tomatoes[1]	0.102	9.6	-4.4	10.4	9.3	-4.4
Other fresh vegetables	0.251	1.9	0.7	-0.4	2.4	-2.8
Processed fruits and vegetables[2]	0.303	0.2	1.7	-0.3	0.5	-0.2
Canned fruits and vegetables[2]	0.157	-0.2	1.7	-0.7	0.7	0.0
Canned fruits[2, 3]		1.1	2.0	-0.5	1.0	0.6
Canned vegetables[2, 3]		-0.3	1.5	-1.2	0.8	-0.2
Frozen fruits and vegetables[2]	0.088	0.6	1.2	-0.4	1.1	-0.9
Frozen vegetables[3]		1.0	2.3	-1.0	1.3	-0.2
Other processed fruits and vegetables including dried[2]	0.057	0.7	2.5	-0.1	0.4	1.0
Dried beans, peas, and lentils[1, 2, 3]		3.8	-1.3	1.0	1.1	-1.3
Nonalcoholic beverages and beverage materials	0.955	0.9	1.0	0.5	-0.4	0.1
Juices and nonalcoholic drinks[2]	0.699	0.0	0.7	0.5	-0.4	-0.3
Carbonated drinks	0.285	0.0	1.4	-0.1	0.4	-1.1
Frozen noncarbonated juices and drinks[1, 2]	0.014	2.3	0.2	0.6	0.0	0.2
Nonfrozen noncarbonated juices and drinks[2]	0.400	0.0	0.2	1.0	-0.8	0.0
Beverage materials including coffee and tea[2]	0.256	3.5	1.8	0.1	-0.1	0.7
Coffee	0.158	6.1	3.1	0.2	0.1	1.4
Roasted coffee[3]		6.7	4.0	0.3	0.3	2.0
Instant and freeze dried coffee[1, 3]		2.9	-0.1	-0.8	1.9	-0.1
Other beverage materials including tea[2]	0.099	-0.5	-0.3	0.8	-0.5	-1.1
Other food at home	2.043	1.3	0.2	0.2	0.2	-0.1
Sugar and sweets[1]	0.299	2.0	1.9	-0.2	0.5	1.9
Sugar and artificial sweeteners	0.054	0.9	4.7	0.9	0.5	2.1
Candy and chewing gum[1, 2]	0.185	2.9	0.9	0.1	0.6	0.9
Other sweets[2]	0.060	0.1	2.4	1.0	-0.2	0.4
Fats and oils	0.245	0.8	0.8	-0.8	-0.4	-0.6
Butter and margarine[2]	0.077	8.8	0.6	-0.6	-1.3	-1.5
Butter[3]		19.5	0.8	-1.3	-2.3	-2.5
Margarine[3]		-0.4	0.0	0.1	0.2	-2.6
Salad dressing[2]	0.062	-2.1	0.7	-1.1	0.0	0.6
Other fats and oils including peanut butter[2]	0.107	-2.7	1.0	-0.5	-0.1	-0.5
Peanut butter[1, 2, 3]		-5.1	-1.3	-0.6	-0.3	-1.3
Other foods	1.499	1.2	-0.3	0.4	0.3	-0.5

See footnotes at end of table.

Table 2. Consumer Price Index for All Urban Consumers (CPI-U): U.S. city average, by detailed expenditure category, January 2015 — Continued
[1982-84=100, unless otherwise noted]

Expenditure category	Relative importance Dec. 2014	Unadjusted percent change		Seasonally adjusted percent change		
		Jan. 2014-Jan. 2015	Dec. 2014-Jan. 2015	Oct. 2014-Nov. 2014	Nov. 2014-Dec. 2014	Dec. 2014-Jan. 2015
Soups....................................	0.093	-1.6	0.7	0.3	-0.5	-0.6
Frozen and freeze dried prepared foods[1]..........	0.285	2.3	-1.4	1.2	0.3	-1.4
Snacks[1]...	0.330	1.0	-0.7	0.1	0.4	-0.7
Spices, seasonings, condiments, sauces...........	0.292	1.9	2.1	0.1	0.8	-0.4
Salt and other seasonings and spices[2,3].......		2.4	1.9	1.9	0.3	-1.3
Olives, pickles, relishes[1,2,3].....................		0.4	0.1	-2.2	1.0	0.1
Sauces and gravies[2,3]...........................		3.2	1.9	-0.5	1.0	1.3
Other condiments[3]................................		1.2	3.5	0.4	1.0	-0.6
Baby food[1,2]..	0.055	1.9	-0.2	0.0	-0.1	-0.2
Other miscellaneous foods[1,2]......................	0.444	0.9	-0.9	1.0	0.5	-0.9
Prepared salads[1,3,4]...........................		3.4	-0.8	0.9	1.0	-0.8
Food away from home[1]..................................	5.830	3.1	0.2	0.4	0.3	0.2
Full service meals and snacks[1,2].....................	2.823	3.0	0.1	0.3	0.2	0.1
Limited service meals and snacks[1,2].................	2.413	3.4	0.3	0.5	0.3	0.3
Food at employee sites and schools[2].................	0.212	1.9	0.1	0.2	0.1	0.1
Food at elementary and secondary schools[3,5].........		2.3	0.0	0.2	0.0	0.1
Food from vending machines and mobile vendors[1,2]....	0.064	1.7	0.8	0.7	0.6	0.8
Other food away from home[1,2].........................	0.319	2.2	0.0	0.2	0.2	0.0
Energy...	8.030	-19.6	-8.2	-4.1	-4.7	-9.7
Energy commodities.................................	4.215	-34.7	-16.5	-7.0	-9.0	-18.0
Fuel oil and other fuels[1].............................	0.236	-24.9	-7.1	-2.0	-4.9	-7.1
Fuel oil[1]...	0.139	-29.7	-9.9	-3.5	-7.8	-9.9
Propane, kerosene, and firewood[1,6].............	0.097	-17.4	-3.0	-1.9	-2.1	-7.7
Motor fuel...	3.979	-35.2	-17.1	-7.2	-9.2	-18.6
Gasoline (all types)..................................	3.904	-35.4	-17.1	-7.2	-9.2	-18.7
Gasoline, unleaded regular[3]......................		-36.2	-17.6	-7.4	-9.5	-19.1
Gasoline, unleaded midgrade[3,7]................		-34.0	-16.3	-6.5	-9.4	-18.1
Gasoline, unleaded premium[3]...................		-31.3	-14.9	-4.5	-6.7	-16.4
Other motor fuels[2]...............................	0.075	-24.2	-13.4	-1.4	-3.7	-13.5
Energy services[8].....................................	3.815	1.9	1.0	-0.3	0.8	-0.1
Electricity[8]..	2.940	2.5	1.9	0.0	0.6	0.9
Utility (piped) gas service[8]......................	0.875	-0.4	-2.0	-1.3	1.4	-3.4
All items less food and energy...............................	77.713	1.6	0.2	0.1	0.1	0.2
Commodities less food and energy commodities............	19.408	-0.8	-0.2	-0.3	-0.2	-0.1
Household furnishings and supplies[9]......................	3.342	-2.1	0.1	-0.3	-0.3	-0.3
Window and floor coverings and other linens[1,2]........	0.266	-4.0	1.1	-0.6	-2.5	1.1
Floor coverings[1,2].................................	0.047	1.3	0.8	-0.7	-0.2	0.8
Window coverings[1,2]................................	0.053	-4.4	-1.7	3.4	-3.3	-1.7
Other linens[1,2].....................................	0.166	-5.3	2.0	-1.9	-2.8	2.0
Furniture and bedding[1]....................................	0.769	-2.2	-0.5	0.1	0.3	-0.5
Bedroom furniture[1].....................................	0.268	-4.2	-1.4	-0.2	-0.3	-1.4
Living room, kitchen, and dining room furniture[1,2]...	0.363	-1.5	0.1	0.3	0.7	0.1
Other furniture[2].......................................	0.128	0.3	-0.1	-0.7	0.2	-0.2
Infants' furniture[1,3,5]...............................						
Appliances[2]...	0.271	-4.9	1.2	-1.1	-0.6	0.1
Major appliances[2].....................................	0.147	-7.7	1.4	-1.8	0.0	-0.4
Laundry equipment[3]................................		-8.4	0.9	-3.7	1.2	0.0
Other appliances[1,2]..................................	0.120	-1.3	1.0	-0.1	-2.1	1.0
Other household equipment and furnishings[2]..........	0.479	-3.3	0.5	-1.2	-0.9	-0.3
Clocks, lamps, and decorator items[1]...................	0.257	-4.3	0.7	-1.8	-1.6	0.7
Indoor plants and flowers[10]...........................	0.107	1.6	0.0	0.7	0.2	0.2
Dishes and flatware[1,2]................................	0.041	-6.6	3.4	-3.8	-3.6	3.4
Nonelectric cookware and tableware[2].................	0.074	-4.1	-0.8	-1.2	-0.4	-1.5

See footnotes at end of table.

Table 2. Consumer Price Index for All Urban Consumers (CPI-U): U.S. city average, by detailed expenditure category, January 2015 — Continued
[1982-84=100, unless otherwise noted]

Expenditure category	Relative importance Dec. 2014	Unadjusted percent change		Seasonally adjusted percent change		
		Jan. 2014- Jan. 2015	Dec. 2014- Jan. 2015	Oct. 2014- Nov. 2014	Nov. 2014- Dec. 2014	Dec. 2014- Jan. 2015
Tools, hardware, outdoor equipment and supplies[2]....	0.710	-0.6	0.0	0.0	0.1	-0.6
Tools, hardware and supplies[1, 2]......................	0.189	0.8	0.0	-0.5	0.4	0.0
Outdoor equipment and supplies[2].....................	0.367	-1.3	0.0	-0.1	0.1	-0.8
Housekeeping supplies[1]............................	0.847	-1.1	-0.4	-0.3	-0.1	-0.4
Household cleaning products[2].........................	0.337	-2.0	-0.9	0.1	0.0	-0.7
Household paper products[1, 2].........................	0.247	-1.1	-0.6	-0.6	-0.3	-0.6
Miscellaneous household products[1, 2]................	0.263	-0.1	0.4	-0.8	-0.4	0.4
Apparel..	3.343	-1.4	-1.1	-0.7	-0.8	0.3
Men's and boys' apparel...............................	0.834	-2.2	0.3	-0.2	-0.7	0.1
Men's apparel....................................	0.653	-2.4	0.2	-0.1	-1.0	-0.5
Men's suits, sport coats, and outerwear............	0.104	-5.4	1.1	-1.3	-1.7	1.2
Men's furnishings.................................	0.185	-4.4	-1.6	-0.5	-1.0	-2.5
Men's shirts and sweaters[2]........................	0.196	-5.4	-2.3	-0.4	-1.3	-1.5
Men's pants and shorts...........................	0.160	5.8	4.8	0.6	-0.5	1.4
Boys' apparel...................................	0.181	-1.2	0.7	-1.1	-0.1	2.1
Women's and girls' apparel...........................	1.439	-2.9	-2.2	-1.1	-1.6	0.8
Women's apparel..................................	1.210	-3.5	-2.6	-0.9	-1.2	0.0
Women's outerwear...............................	0.118	6.2	-4.4	-2.7	-0.8	3.3
Women's dresses.................................	0.155	-2.1	-7.6	0.3	-0.8	-2.6
Women's suits and separates[2].....................	0.550	-7.7	-3.0	-1.6	-1.1	-1.2
Women's underwear, nightwear, sportswear and accessories[2]................	0.378	-0.4	0.5	-0.9	-0.4	0.0
Girls' apparel....................................	0.229	0.7	0.0	-1.9	-3.5	4.9
Footwear..	0.725	2.6	-1.8	-0.5	0.4	-0.7
Men's footwear[1].................................	0.218	0.1	0.2	-0.6	-1.0	0.2
Boys' and girls' footwear...........................	0.178	5.4	-3.4	-1.7	0.2	-1.8
Women's footwear................................	0.329	2.8	-2.2	-0.5	0.6	-0.9
Infants' and toddlers' apparel.........................	0.135	0.8	-1.2	-0.4	0.0	0.0
Jewelry and watches[6]..............................	0.211	-2.8	2.6	-0.6	-0.7	0.7
Watches[1, 6].....................................	0.046	2.3	2.6	-2.5	-1.3	2.6
Jewelry[6].......................................	0.164	-4.1	2.7	-0.4	-0.4	0.1
Transportation commodities less motor fuel[9]..............	5.685	-0.9	-0.1	-0.3	-0.2	-0.1
New vehicles....................................	3.551	0.5	0.0	0.0	0.0	-0.1
New cars and trucks[2, 3]..........................		0.5	0.0	0.0	0.0	-0.1
New cars[3].....................................		-0.2	0.0	0.0	-0.1	-0.1
New trucks[3, 11].................................		1.1	0.0	0.0	0.0	-0.4
Used cars and trucks..............................	1.591	-4.0	-0.3	0.9	-0.8	-0.1
Motor vehicle parts and equipment[1]..................	0.435	-0.4	0.2	-0.2	0.4	0.2
Tires[1]...	0.285	-1.3	0.3	-0.4	0.5	0.3
Vehicle accessories other than tires[1, 2].............	0.150	1.5	-0.1	0.1	0.3	-0.1
Vehicle parts and equipment other than tires[1, 3].................................		1.0	-0.3	0.3	0.2	-0.3
Motor oil, coolant, and fluids[1, 3]...................		2.4	-0.3	-0.5	0.8	-0.3
Medical care commodities...........................	1.772	3.9	0.1	0.6	0.9	-0.3
Medicinal drugs[1, 9]..............................	1.696	4.2	0.1	0.4	0.6	0.1
Prescription drugs................................	1.345	5.6	0.4	0.6	0.7	-0.2
Nonprescription drugs[1, 9]........................	0.351	-1.1	-1.0	0.2	0.4	-1.0
Medical equipment and supplies[1, 9]................	0.076	-1.0	-1.5	0.0	-0.1	-1.5
Recreation commodities[9]...........................	2.007	-2.8	-0.2	-0.6	-0.3	-0.5
Video and audio products[9].........................	0.289	-10.3	0.3	-2.0	-1.3	-0.4
Televisions....................................	0.133	-16.7	-0.1	-3.0	-1.9	-0.9
Other video equipment[1, 2].......................	0.029	1.2	2.0	-2.7	-4.5	2.0
Audio equipment...............................	0.066	-7.9	0.1	-1.2	0.0	-1.0
Audio discs, tapes and other media[1, 2]............	0.044	-2.8	0.4	-0.1	0.7	0.4

See footnotes at end of table.

Table 2. Consumer Price Index for All Urban Consumers (CPI-U): U.S. city average, by detailed expenditure category, January 2015 — Continued
[1982-84=100, unless otherwise noted]

Expenditure category	Relative importance Dec. 2014	Unadjusted percent change		Seasonally adjusted percent change		
		Jan. 2014- Jan. 2015	Dec. 2014- Jan. 2015	Oct. 2014- Nov. 2014	Nov. 2014- Dec. 2014	Dec. 2014- Jan. 2015
Pets and pet products[1]	0.659	-0.3	-0.8	0.1	0.1	-0.8
Pet food[1, 2, 3]		-0.4	-1.1	0.0	0.1	-1.1
Purchase of pets, pet supplies, accessories[1, 2, 3]		0.1	-0.6	0.3	0.1	-0.6
Sporting goods[1]	0.400	-1.9	0.1	-0.8	-0.8	0.1
Sports vehicles including bicycles[1]	0.181	-0.8	0.6	-0.6	-0.4	0.6
Sports equipment	0.214	-2.8	-0.3	-0.4	-0.6	-0.2
Photographic equipment and supplies	0.058	-4.3	-1.3	-0.4	-0.9	-1.8
Film and photographic supplies[1, 2, 3]		14.7	-0.2	0.9	-1.2	-0.2
Photographic equipment[2, 3]		-7.3	-1.3	-0.8	-1.3	-1.7
Recreational reading materials[1]	0.220	2.1	0.1	-0.3	0.1	0.1
Newspapers and magazines[1, 2]	0.123	4.6	-0.4	-0.4	0.9	-0.4
Recreational books[1, 2]	0.094	-0.9	0.7	-0.1	-0.8	0.7
Other recreational goods[2]	0.381	-4.2	0.2	-0.6	-0.1	-0.9
Toys	0.277	-5.3	0.6	-0.8	0.3	-0.8
Toys, games, hobbies and playground equipment[2, 3]		-2.4	1.2	-0.2	0.3	-0.2
Sewing machines, fabric and supplies[1, 2]	0.050	-2.6	-1.2	0.0	-2.0	-1.2
Music instruments and accessories[2]	0.042	1.1	-1.2	0.1	-0.1	-1.2
Education and communication commodities[9]	0.610	-4.4	0.0	-0.8	-0.6	-0.5
Educational books and supplies	0.203	6.5	0.7	0.3	0.9	0.3
College textbooks[1, 3, 12]		7.4	0.8	-0.1	0.7	0.8
Information technology commodities[9]	0.408	-9.1	-0.3	-1.3	-1.3	-0.9
Personal computers and peripheral equipment[4]	0.272	-10.4	-0.4	-1.3	-1.6	-1.3
Computer software and accessories[1, 2]	0.068	-1.8	-0.6	0.4	-1.3	-0.6
Telephone hardware, calculators, and other consumer information items[1, 2]	0.068	-10.6	0.1	-2.9	-0.3	0.1
Alcoholic beverages	1.015	1.0	-0.1	0.6	-0.3	-0.3
Alcoholic beverages at home	0.597	0.1	-0.1	0.8	-0.4	-0.6
Beer, ale, and other malt beverages at home	0.274	0.2	-0.2	0.4	-0.3	-0.4
Distilled spirits at home[1]	0.073	0.5	0.5	0.4	0.0	-0.4
Whiskey at home[1, 3]		2.0	0.7	-0.5	0.1	0.7
Distilled spirits, excluding whiskey, at home[3]		0.1	0.2	0.6	0.3	-0.7
Wine at home	0.250	-0.1	-0.1	1.0	-0.5	-0.7
Alcoholic beverages away from home[1]	0.418	2.3	0.0	0.5	0.0	0.0
Beer, ale, and other malt beverages away from home[1, 2, 3]		1.8	-0.1	0.6	-0.1	-0.1
Wine away from home[1, 2, 3]		2.4	0.0	0.7	0.0	0.0
Distilled spirits away from home[1, 2, 3]		2.6	0.0	0.4	0.0	0.0
Other goods[9]	1.634	1.5	0.5	-0.4	0.1	0.4
Tobacco and smoking products	0.718	2.4	0.1	0.3	0.4	-0.2
Cigarettes[2]	0.661	2.5	0.2	0.2	0.5	-0.1
Tobacco products other than cigarettes[1, 2]	0.050	0.6	-1.2	0.4	0.5	-1.2
Personal care products[1]	0.724	1.3	1.2	-0.8	-0.2	1.2
Hair, dental, shaving, and miscellaneous personal care products[1, 2]	0.369	0.5	1.2	-0.6	-0.2	1.2
Cosmetics, perfume, bath, nail preparations and implements[1]	0.348	2.1	1.2	-1.0	-0.2	1.2
Miscellaneous personal goods[2]	0.192	-0.6	-0.3	-1.3	0.2	-0.2
Stationery, stationery supplies, gift wrap[3]		-0.8	-1.3	-1.1	0.0	-0.9
Infants' equipment[1, 3, 5]		-1.3	-1.9	-0.6	0.5	-1.9
Services less energy services	58.305	2.5	0.3	0.2	0.2	0.3
Shelter	32.711	2.9	0.4	0.2	0.2	0.3
Rent of shelter[13]	32.336	2.9	0.4	0.2	0.2	0.3
Rent of primary residence[8]	7.159	3.4	0.2	0.3	0.2	0.2

See footnotes at end of table.

Table 2. Consumer Price Index for All Urban Consumers (CPI-U): U.S. city average, by detailed expenditure category, January 2015 — Continued
[1982-84=100, unless otherwise noted]

Expenditure category	Relative importance Dec. 2014	Unadjusted percent change		Seasonally adjusted percent change		
		Jan. 2014- Jan. 2015	Dec. 2014- Jan. 2015	Oct. 2014- Nov. 2014	Nov. 2014- Dec. 2014	Dec. 2014- Jan. 2015
Lodging away from home[2]	0.839	6.6	4.6	0.3	0.4	1.3
Housing at school, excluding board[8, 13]	0.172	2.7	0.1	0.2	0.3	0.3
Other lodging away from home including hotels and motels	0.666	7.6	5.7	0.3	0.4	1.5
Owners' equivalent rent of residences[8, 13]	24.339	2.6	0.2	0.2	0.2	0.2
Owners' equivalent rent of primary residence[8, 13]	22.918	2.6	0.2	0.2	0.2	0.2
Tenants' and household insurance[1, 2]	0.375	5.6	0.7	0.1	0.9	0.7
Water and sewer and trash collection services[2]	1.222	4.5	0.4	0.5	0.5	0.1
Water and sewerage maintenance[8]	0.945	5.5	0.5	0.7	0.6	0.2
Garbage and trash collection[1, 11]	0.277	1.3	-0.1	0.0	0.1	-0.1
Household operations[1, 2]	0.848	3.0	0.2	0.0	-0.3	0.2
Domestic services[1, 2]	0.279	1.7	0.3	0.2	0.1	0.3
Gardening and lawncare services[1, 2]	0.279		-0.2	0.0	0.0	-0.2
Moving, storage, freight expense[2]	0.116	2.9	1.1	-0.6	-0.9	1.1
Repair of household items[1, 2]	0.066	4.4	0.3	0.1	0.8	0.3
Medical care services	5.944	2.3	0.3	0.3	0.3	0.1
Professional services	3.032	1.7	0.2	0.4	0.1	0.0
Physicians' services[8]	1.590	1.7	0.3	0.4	0.2	0.1
Dental services[8]	0.804	2.2	0.8	0.2	0.0	0.5
Eyeglasses and eye care[1, 6]	0.284	1.4	-0.8	0.6	0.1	-0.8
Services by other medical professionals[8, 6]	0.354	1.1	-0.6	0.8	0.0	-0.8
Hospital and related services	2.159	4.1	0.6	0.3	0.5	0.2
Hospital services[8, 14]	1.853	4.3	0.6	0.3	0.5	0.2
Inpatient hospital services[8, 14, 3]		4.3	0.5	0.2	0.7	-0.1
Outpatient hospital services[8, 3, 6]		4.4	0.7	0.1	0.5	0.4
Nursing homes and adult day services[8, 14]	0.174	3.4	1.0	0.3	0.2	0.3
Care of invalids and elderly at home[1, 5]	0.132	1.8	0.2	0.1	0.4	0.2
Health insurance[1, 5]	0.753	-0.5	0.2	0.1	0.1	0.2
Transportation services	5.625	2.1	0.0	0.2	0.0	0.4
Leased cars and trucks[12]	0.397	0.8	0.3	-0.1	0.5	0.7
Car and truck rental[2]	0.073	1.4	1.2	1.3	-0.6	3.7
Motor vehicle maintenance and repair[1]	1.168	2.0	0.1	0.1	0.1	0.1
Motor vehicle body work[1]	0.057	1.9	0.2	0.1	0.3	0.2
Motor vehicle maintenance and servicing[1]	0.492	1.6	-0.2	0.7	0.0	-0.2
Motor vehicle repair[1, 2]	0.587	2.3	0.4	-0.4	0.1	0.4
Motor vehicle insurance	2.300	5.0	0.5	0.3	0.3	0.6
Motor vehicle fees[1, 2]	0.565	0.1	0.1	0.1	0.1	0.1
State motor vehicle registration and license fees[1, 8, 2]	0.312	-1.2	0.1	-0.2	0.0	0.1
Parking and other fees[2]	0.235	1.7	0.1	0.5	0.3	-0.5
Parking fees and tolls[1, 2, 3]		2.3	0.2	0.3	0.7	0.2
Automobile service clubs[1, 2, 3]		-0.4	0.5	-0.1	-0.1	0.5
Public transportation	1.122	-1.8	-1.2	0.0	-1.1	-0.1
Airline fare	0.702	-3.0	-1.4	-0.2	-2.0	-0.3
Other intercity transportation	0.157	-1.6	-2.8	1.3	-0.4	-0.9
Intercity bus fare[1, 3, 4]						
Intercity train fare[1, 3, 4]		1.6	-6.2	4.0	5.6	-6.2
Ship fare[1, 2, 3]		-1.1	0.4	2.2	0.3	0.4
Intracity transportation[1]	0.260	1.4	0.3	0.0	0.0	0.3
Intracity mass transit[1, 3, 9]		1.1	0.1	0.0	0.0	0.1
Recreation services[9]	3.744	1.6	0.7	0.0	0.2	0.5
Video and audio services[9]	1.558	1.8	0.5	-0.1	0.3	0.1

See footnotes at end of table.

Table 2. Consumer Price Index for All Urban Consumers (CPI-U): U.S. city average, by detailed expenditure category, January 2015 — Continued

[1982-84=100, unless otherwise noted]

Expenditure category	Relative importance Dec. 2014	Unadjusted percent change		Seasonally adjusted percent change		
		Jan. 2014- Jan. 2015	Dec. 2014- Jan. 2015	Oct. 2014- Nov. 2014	Nov. 2014- Dec. 2014	Dec. 2014- Jan. 2015
Cable and satellite television and radio service[11]	1.468	2.1	0.4	-0.1	0.3	0.1
Video discs and other media, including rental of video and audio[1, 2]	0.090	-2.6	1.4	-0.9	-1.2	1.4
Video discs and other media[1, 2, 3]		-6.3	1.7	-2.4	-2.7	1.7
Rental of video or audio discs and other media[1, 2, 3]		2.5	1.2	0.1	1.2	1.2
Pet services including veterinary[2]	0.399	2.9	0.7	0.3	0.2	0.6
Pet services[1, 2, 3]		1.8	0.3	0.2	0.0	0.3
Veterinarian services[2, 3]		3.2	0.7	0.3	0.2	0.6
Photographers and film processing[1, 2]	0.062	2.1	0.1	-0.1	0.2	0.1
Photographer fees[1, 2, 3]		1.1	0.0	-1.3	0.1	0.0
Film processing[1, 2, 3]		4.0	0.7	0.0	0.4	0.7
Other recreation services[2]	1.724	1.1	0.8	0.0	0.0	0.8
Club dues and fees for participant sports and group exercises[2]	0.602	0.6	1.4	0.0	-0.6	1.4
Admissions[1]	0.640	0.9	0.6	0.0	0.7	0.6
Admission to movies, theaters, and concerts[1, 2, 3]		0.2	0.1	-0.4	0.6	0.1
Admission to sporting events[1, 2, 3]		3.6	1.8	0.0	1.2	1.8
Fees for lessons or instructions[1, 6]	0.211	2.0	0.1	0.0	0.0	0.1
Education and communication services[9]	6.452	0.9	0.2	0.0	0.0	0.2
Tuition, other school fees, and childcare	3.122	3.5	0.3	0.3	0.2	0.5
College tuition and fees	1.853	3.6	0.2	0.3	0.3	0.4
Elementary and high school tuition and fees	0.377	4.0	0.0	0.3	0.3	0.3
Child care and nursery school[10]	0.725	3.0	0.7	0.2	0.1	0.5
Technical and business school tuition and fees[2]	0.039	2.0	0.0	0.3	0.2	0.2
Postage and delivery services[2]	0.144	3.4	0.3	0.3	0.3	-0.5
Postage[1]	0.130	3.6	0.0	0.4	0.4	-0.5
Delivery services[2]	0.014	1.9	3.5	-0.5	0.0	0.1
Telephone services[1, 2]	2.462	-2.5	0.0	-0.4	-0.2	0.0
Wireless telephone services[1, 2]	1.624	-4.3	-0.5	-0.6	-0.5	-0.5
Land-line telephone services[1, 9]	0.837	1.1	0.8	-0.1	0.3	0.8
Internet services and electronic information providers[2]	0.711	1.8	0.2	0.1	-0.2	0.2
Other personal services[1, 9]	1.760	2.1	0.4	0.1	0.2	0.4
Personal care services[1]	0.638	1.4	-0.1	0.1	0.5	-0.1
Haircuts and other personal care services[1, 2]	0.638	1.4	-0.1	0.1	0.5	-0.1
Miscellaneous personal services	1.122	2.5	0.7	0.2	0.2	0.6
Legal services[6]	0.316	1.2	0.2	0.0	-0.2	0.2
Funeral expenses[1, 6]	0.173	1.4	0.3	0.1	0.0	0.3
Laundry and dry cleaning services[1, 2]	0.276	2.2	0.2	0.2	0.0	0.2
Apparel services other than laundry and dry cleaning[1, 2]	0.034	2.0	0.4	0.1	-0.2	0.4
Financial services[1, 6]	0.228	5.7	2.2	0.5	0.3	2.2
Checking account and other bank services[1, 2, 3]		0.1	0.1	0.0	0.2	0.1
Tax return preparation and other accounting fees[2, 3]		9.3	3.2	0.6	0.2	3.2

[1] Not seasonally adjusted.
[2] Indexes on a December 1997=100 base.
[3] Special index based on a substantially smaller sample.
[4] Indexes on a December 2007=100 base.
[5] Indexes on a December 2005=100 base.
[6] Indexes on a December 1986=100 base.
[7] Indexes on a December 1993=100 base.

[8] This index series was calculated using a Laspeyres estimator. All other item stratum index series were calculated using a geometric means estimator.

[9] Indexes on a December 2009=100 base.

[10] Indexes on a December 1990=100 base.

[11] Indexes on a December 1983=100 base.

[12] Indexes on a December 2001=100 base.

[13] Indexes on a December 1982=100 base.

[14] Indexes on a December 1996=100 base.

NOTE: Index applies to a month as a whole, not to any specific date.

Table 3. Consumer Price Index for All Urban Consumers (CPI-U): U.S. city average, special aggregate indexes, January 2015

[1982-84=100, unless otherwise noted]

Special aggregate indexes	Relative importance Dec. 2014	Unadjusted indexes			Unadjusted percent change		Seasonally adjusted percent change		
		Jan. 2014	Dec. 2014	Jan. 2015	Jan. 2014- Jan. 2015	Dec. 2014- Jan. 2015	Oct. 2014- Nov. 2014	Nov. 2014- Dec. 2014	Dec. 2014- Jan. 2015
All items less food.................................	85.743	233.161	233.079	231.711	-0.6	-0.6	-0.4	-0.4	-0.8
All items less shelter..............................	67.289	223.710	222.267	220.322	-1.5	-0.9	-0.5	-0.6	-1.1
All items less food and shelter.....................	53.032	219.567	216.110	213.576	-2.7	-1.2	-0.7	-0.8	-1.4
All items less food, shelter, and energy..........	45.002	218.112	219.531	219.704	0.7	0.1	0.0	0.0	0.1
All items less food, shelter, energy, and used cars and trucks...................................	43.411	222.367	224.183	224.394	0.9	0.1	0.0	0.0	0.1
All items less medical care........................	92.284	224.423	224.921	223.721	-0.3	-0.5	-0.3	-0.4	-0.7
All items less energy...............................	91.970	235.230	239.186	239.670	1.9	0.2	0.1	0.1	0.1
Commodities..	37.880	186.152	181.926	178.576	-4.1	-1.8	-1.0	-1.2	-2.2
Commodities less food, energy, and used cars and trucks..................................	17.817	146.595	146.109	145.868	-0.5	-0.2	-0.2	-0.2	-0.1
Commodities less food..........................	23.623	161.354	152.990	148.260	-8.1	-3.1	-1.7	-2.0	-3.5
Commodities less food and beverages........	22.608	158.602	149.965	145.124	-8.5	-3.2	-1.8	-2.1	-3.6
Services...	62.120	281.299	287.129	288.178	2.4	0.4	0.2	0.2	0.2
Services less rent of shelter[1]....................	29.784	307.124	311.948	313.112	1.9	0.4	0.1	0.2	0.1
Services less medical care services...........	56.176	267.746	273.341	274.345	2.5	0.4	0.2	0.2	0.2
Durables...	8.950	110.697	108.500	108.474	-2.0	0.0	-0.4	-0.3	-0.2
Nondurables...	28.930	223.630	218.358	213.108	-4.7	-2.4	-0.7	-1.0	-2.9
Nondurables less food...........................	14.673	209.328	194.603	184.946	-11.6	-5.0	-1.6	-2.2	-5.6
Nondurables less food and beverages........	13.658	207.582	191.838	181.619	-12.5	-5.3	-1.8	-2.4	-6.0
Nondurables less food, beverages, and apparel.....................................	10.315	264.205	238.493	222.554	-15.8	-6.7	-2.1	-2.8	-7.9
Nondurables less food and apparel............	11.330	260.427	237.355	222.900	-14.4	-6.1	-1.8	-2.6	-7.2
Housing...	42.173	230.256	234.658	235.485	2.3	0.4	0.1	0.2	0.1
Education and communication[2]...................	7.062	137.005	137.410	137.604	0.4	0.1	-0.1	0.0	0.2
Education[2]...	3.325	228.373	236.066	236.820	3.7	0.3	0.3	0.3	0.5
Communication[2]................................	3.737	82.571	80.681	80.667	-2.3	0.0	-0.4	-0.3	-0.1
Information and information processing[2]....	3.593	78.809	76.846	76.822	-2.5	0.0	-0.4	-0.4	-0.1
Information technology, hardware and services[3]......................................	1.132	8.389	8.182	8.181	-2.5	0.0	0.0	0.0	-1.1
Recreation[2]..	5.750	115.275	114.875	115.288	0.0	0.4	-0.2	0.0	0.2
Video and audio[2]................................	1.847	99.444	98.702	99.144	-0.3	0.4	-0.5	0.5	-0.4
Pets, pet products and services[2]...............	1.058	164.944	166.919	166.468	0.9	-0.3	0.2	0.2	-0.3
Photography[2].....................................	0.120	76.426	76.047	75.631	-1.0	-0.5	-0.3	-0.4	-0.8
Food and beverages................................	15.272	238.792	245.585	246.100	3.1	0.2	0.2	0.2	-0.1
Domestically produced farm food..............	7.094	242.785	251.370	251.845	3.7	0.2	0.1	0.5	-0.4
Other services......................................	11.955	332.006	335.162	336.331	1.3	0.3	0.0	0.1	0.3
Apparel less footwear.............................	2.619	118.336	116.574	115.448	-2.4	-1.0	-0.7	-1.2	0.5
Fuels and utilities..................................	5.273	230.098	231.150	232.309	1.0	0.5	-0.2	0.5	-0.4
Household energy...............................	4.051	198.266	197.092	198.143	-0.1	0.5	-0.4	0.4	-0.5
Medical care..	7.716	429.621	439.720	440.969	2.6	0.3	0.4	0.4	0.0
Transportation......................................	15.289	213.450	199.777	190.871	-10.6	-4.5	-2.3	-2.8	-5.0
Private transportation...........................	14.167	208.925	194.641	185.461	-11.2	-4.7	-2.4	-2.9	-5.4
New and used motor vehicles[2]..............	5.720	100.284	99.544	99.498	-0.8	0.0	-0.3	-0.2	0.0
Utilities and public transportation..................	10.089	213.203	213.925	214.665	0.7	0.3	-0.1	0.1	0.0
Household furnishings and operations...........	4.189	123.735	122.237	122.351	-1.1	0.1	-0.3	-0.3	-0.2
Other goods and services.........................	3.394	405.127	410.642	412.545	1.8	0.5	-0.1	0.2	0.4
Personal care.....................................	2.676	216.414	218.850	220.071	1.7	0.6	-0.2	0.1	0.6

[1] Indexes on a December 1982=100 base.
[2] Indexes on a December 1997=100 base.
[3] Indexes on a December 1988=100 base.
NOTE: Index applies to a month as a whole, not to any specific date.

Table 4. Consumer Price Index for All Urban Consumers (CPI-U): Selected areas, all items index, January 2015
[1982-84=100, unless otherwise noted]

Area	Pricing Schedule[1]	Percent change to Jan. 2015 from:			Percent change to Dec. 2014 from:		
		Jan. 2014	Nov. 2014	Dec. 2014	Dec. 2013	Oct. 2014	Nov. 2014
U.S. city average...	M	-0.1	-1.0	-0.5	0.8	-1.1	-0.6
Region and area size[2]							
Northeast urban...	M	-0.4	-0.7	-0.2	0.4	-0.9	-0.5
Size A - More than 1,500,000..........................	M	-0.2	-0.6	-0.1	0.6	-0.7	-0.5
Size B/C - 50,000 to 1,500,000[3]......................	M	-1.1	-1.0	-0.4	-0.1	-1.4	-0.6
Midwest urban...	M	-0.3	-1.3	-0.6	0.7	-1.3	-0.7
Size A - More than 1,500,000..........................	M	-0.3	-1.2	-0.5	0.7	-1.3	-0.7
Size B/C - 50,000 to 1,500,000[3]......................	M	-0.2	-1.4	-0.7	0.9	-1.3	-0.7
Size D - Nonmetropolitan (less than 50,000).........	M	-0.9	-1.4	-0.6	0.0	-1.5	-0.8
South urban..	M	-0.4	-1.3	-0.7	0.6	-1.2	-0.6
Size A - More than 1,500,000..........................	M	-0.1	-1.1	-0.6	0.7	-0.9	-0.5
Size B/C - 50,000 to 1,500,000[3]......................	M	-0.6	-1.5	-0.8	0.4	-1.3	-0.7
Size D - Nonmetropolitan (less than 50,000).........	M	0.2	-1.2	-0.6	1.3	-1.3	-0.6
West urban...	M	0.7	-0.8	-0.3	1.3	-1.1	-0.5
Size A - More than 1,500,000..........................	M	0.9	-0.7	-0.2	1.4	-1.0	-0.5
Size B/C - 50,000 to 1,500,000[3]......................	M	0.0	-1.0	-0.5	0.6	-1.1	-0.5
Size classes							
A[4]...	M	0.1	-0.8	-0.3	0.9	-1.0	-0.5
B/C[3]...	M	-0.5	-1.3	-0.7	0.5	-1.3	-0.7
D..	M	0.1	-1.3	-0.6	1.2	-1.3	-0.6
Selected local areas[5]							
Chicago-Gary-Kenosha, IL-IN-WI..........................	M	0.4	-0.6	-0.2	1.5	-1.2	-0.4
Los Angeles-Riverside-Orange County, CA..............	M	-0.1	-0.8	-0.3	0.7	-1.2	-0.5
New York-Northern N.J.-Long Island, NY-NJ-CT-PA. ..	M	-0.5	-0.4	0.1	0.3	-0.9	-0.5
Boston-Brockton-Nashua, MA-NH-ME-CT................	1	0.6	-0.7				
Cleveland-Akron, OH...	1	0.5	-0.7				
Dallas-Fort Worth, TX..	1	-0.6	-1.1				
Washington-Baltimore, DC-MD-VA-WV[6]..................	1	-0.2	-1.0				
Atlanta, GA..	2				0.9	-1.5	
Detroit-Ann Arbor-Flint, MI...................................	2				-0.1	-1.8	
Houston-Galveston-Brazoria, TX...........................	2				1.1	-1.2	
Miami-Fort Lauderdale, FL...................................	2				1.4	-0.6	
Philadelphia-Wilmington-Atlantic City, PA-NJ-DE-MD...	2				0.6	-0.8	
San Francisco-Oakland-San Jose, CA....................	2				2.7	-0.9	
Seattle-Tacoma-Bremerton, WA............................	2				1.7	-1.1	

[1] Foods, fuels, and several other items are priced every month in all areas. Most other goods and services are priced as indicated: M - Every month. 1 - January, March, May, July, September, and November. 2 - February, April, June, August, October, and December.

[2] Regions defined as the four Census regions.

[3] Indexes on a December 1996=100 base.

[4] Indexes on a December 1986=100 base.

[5] In addition, the following metropolitan areas are published semiannually and appear in Tables 34 and 39 of the January and July issues of the CPI Detailed Report: Anchorage, AK; Cincinnati-Hamilton, OH-KY-IN; Denver-Boulder-Greeley, CO; Honolulu, HI; Kansas City, MO-KS; Milwaukee-Racine, WI; Minneapolis-St. Paul, MN-WI; Phoenix-Mesa, AZ; Pittsburgh, PA; Portland-Salem, OR-WA; St. Louis, MO-IL; San Diego, CA; Tampa-St. Petersburg-Clearwater, FL.

[6] Indexes on a November 1996=100 base.

NOTE: Local area indexes are byproducts of the national CPI program. Each local index has a smaller sample size than the national index and is, therefore, subject to substantially more sampling and other measurement error. As a result, local area indexes show greater volatility than the national index, although their long-term trends are similar. Therefore, the Bureau of Labor Statistics strongly urges users to consider adopting the national average CPI for use in their escalator clauses.

NOTE: Index applies to a month as a whole, not to any specific date.

Table 5. Chained Consumer Price Index for All Urban Consumers (C-CPI-U) and the Consumer Price Index for All Urban Consumers (CPI-U): U.S. city average, all items index, January 2015

[Percent changes]

Month Year	Unadjusted 1-month percent change		Unadjusted 12-month percent change	
	C-CPI-U[1]	CPI-U	C-CPI-U[1]	CPI-U
December 2000............................			2.6	3.4
December 2001............................			1.3	1.6
December 2002............................			2.0	2.4
December 2003............................			1.7	1.9
December 2004............................			3.2	3.3
December 2005............................			2.9	3.4
December 2006............................			2.3	2.5
December 2007............................			3.7	4.1
December 2008............................			0.2	0.1
December 2009............................			2.5	2.7
December 2010............................			1.3	1.5
December 2011............................			2.9	3.0
December 2012............................			1.5	1.7
January 2013..............................	0.3	0.3	1.3	1.6
February 2013.............................	0.8	0.8	1.7	2.0
March 2013................................	0.3	0.3	1.3	1.5
April 2013.................................	-0.1	-0.1	0.9	1.1
May 2013..................................	0.1	0.2	1.1	1.4
June 2013.................................	0.2	0.2	1.5	1.8
July 2013..................................	0.0	0.0	1.7	2.0
August 2013...............................	0.1	0.1	1.3	1.5
September 2013............................	0.1	0.1	1.0	1.2
October 2013..............................	-0.3	-0.3	0.8	1.0
November 2013............................	-0.2	-0.2	1.1	1.2
December 2013............................	-0.1	0.0	1.3	1.5
January 2014..............................	0.4	0.4	1.5	1.6
February 2014.............................	0.4	0.4	1.0	1.1
March 2014................................	0.6	0.6	1.4	1.5
April 2014.................................	0.3	0.3	1.8	2.0
May 2014..................................	0.3	0.3	2.0	2.1
June 2014.................................	0.2	0.2	2.0	2.1
July 2014..................................	-0.1	0.0	1.9	2.0
August 2014...............................	-0.2	-0.2	1.6	1.7
September 2014............................	0.1	0.1	1.5	1.7
October 2014..............................	-0.3	-0.3	1.5	1.7
November 2014............................	-0.6	-0.5	1.1	1.3
December 2014............................	-0.7	-0.6	0.5	0.8
January 2015..............................	-0.7	-0.5	-0.6	-0.1

[1] The C-CPI-U is designed to be a closer approximation to a cost-of-living index in that it, in its final form, accounts for any substitution that consumers make across item categories in response to changes in relative prices. Since the expenditure data required for the calculation of the C-CPI-U are available only with a time lag, the C-CPI-U is being issued first in preliminary form using the latest available expenditure data at that time and is subject to two revisions.

Indexes are issued as initial estimates. Indexes are revised each quarter with the publication of January, April, July, and October data as updated expenditure estimates become available. The C-CPI-U indexes are updated quarterly until they become final. January-March indexes are final in January of the following year; April-June indexes are final in April of the following year; July-September indexes are final in July of the following year; October-December indexes are final in October of the following year.

NOTE: Index applies to a month as a whole, not to any specific date.

Table 6. Consumer Price Index for All Urban Consumers (CPI-U): U.S. city average, by expenditure category, January 2015, 1-month analysis table
[1982-84=100, unless otherwise noted]

Expenditure category	Relative importance Dec. 2014	One Month				
		Seasonally adjusted percent change Dec. 2014-Jan. 2015	Seasonally adjusted effect on All Items Dec. 2014-Jan. 2015[1]	Standard error, median price change[2]	Largest (L) or Smallest (S) seasonally adjusted change since:[3]	
					Date	Percent change
All items...	100.000	-0.7		0.04	S-Dec.2008	-0.8
Food..	14.257	0.0	-0.006	0.08	S-Dec.2013	0.0
Food at home....................................	8.427	-0.2	-0.015	0.12	S-May 2013	-0.4
Cereals and bakery products...........................	1.138	0.7	0.008	0.27	L-Aug.2011	1.0
Cereals and cereal products........................	0.370	1.2	0.004	0.44	L-Sep.2011	1.3
Flour and prepared flour mixes.....................	0.048	2.1	0.001	0.64	L-Apr.2013	2.7
Breakfast cereal[4]...............................	0.197	-0.6	-0.001	0.71	S-Sep.2014	-1.2
Rice, pasta, cornmeal[4]............................	0.126	3.4	0.004	0.67	L-Jul.2008	3.8
Rice[4, 5, 6]..		1.1		0.83	L-May 2014	1.4
Bakery products.....................................	0.767	0.4	0.003	0.31	–	–
Bread[5]...	0.230	-0.2	0.000	0.57	S-Oct.2014	-0.4
White bread[4, 6]...............................		0.2		0.81	S-Nov.2014	-0.2
Bread other than white[4, 6]..................		-1.0		0.88	S-Oct.2014	-1.3
Fresh biscuits, rolls, muffins[4, 5]................	0.116	1.1	0.001	0.69	L-Feb.2014	1.3
Cakes, cupcakes, and cookies....................	0.189	1.3	0.002	0.64	L-Sep.2013	1.4
Cookies[4, 6].....................................		1.5		0.97	L-Aug.2014	1.7
Fresh cakes and cupcakes[4, 6]..............		0.7		0.86	L-Sep.2014	0.8
Other bakery products.............................	0.233	0.2	0.001	0.66	L-Nov.2014	0.2
Fresh sweetrolls, coffeecakes, doughnuts[4, 6]....		0.6		0.84	S-Nov.2014	-0.5
Crackers, bread, and cracker products[6].........		-0.4		1.25	S-Sep.2014	-0.5
Frozen and refrigerated bakery products, pies, tarts, turnovers[6].............................		0.2		0.88	L-Nov.2014	1.0
Meats, poultry, fish, and eggs............................	2.014	-0.1	-0.001	0.22	S-Oct.2014	-0.3
Meats, poultry, and fish.................................	1.880	0.1	0.001	0.24	–	–
Meats...	1.229	0.1	0.001	0.27	S-Oct.2014	0.0
Beef and veal[4]...................................	0.582	0.1	0.001	0.40	S-Jun.2014	0.1
Uncooked ground beef[4]...........................	0.238	1.3	0.003	0.55	L-Nov.2014	1.4
Uncooked beef roasts[4, 5].........................	0.085	-1.1	-0.001	0.87	S-Jan.2014	-1.9
Uncooked beef steaks[4, 5].........................	0.207	-0.7	-0.001	0.70	S-Nov.2014	-0.9
Uncooked other beef and veal[4, 5]................	0.053	-0.2	0.000	0.81	S-Jul.2013	-1.2
Pork...	0.372	-0.4	-0.002	0.47	S-Oct.2014	-0.4
Bacon, breakfast sausage, and related products[5]...........................	0.141	0.3	0.000	0.76	L-May 2014	3.2
Bacon and related products[6]....................		0.0		0.95	L-Sep.2014	0.0
Breakfast sausage and related products[5, 6]...		0.6		0.94	L-Jul.2014	0.7
Ham...	0.078	-1.0	-0.001	0.91	S-Sep.2012	-1.1
Ham, excluding canned[6].......................		-1.3		1.16	S-Sep.2012	-1.4
Pork chops...................................	0.064	-2.0	-0.001	1.17	S-Feb.2014	-2.4
Other pork including roasts and picnics[5].........	0.089	-0.5	0.000	1.01	L-Sep.2014	1.2
Other meats...................................	0.275	0.7	0.002	0.48	L-Sep.2014	1.2
Frankfurters[6]...................................		0.3		1.56	S-Oct.2014	-0.7
Lunchmeats[5, 6]...................................		1.4		0.62	L-Apr.2014	1.4
Lamb and organ meats[4, 6].......................		-0.5		1.72	–	–
Lamb and mutton[4, 5, 6]...........................		0.6		2.54	L-Nov.2014	1.4
Poultry...	0.360	0.5	0.002	0.63	L-Nov.2014	1.4
Chicken[4, 5].....................................	0.294	0.4	0.001	0.76	L-Nov.2014	1.2
Fresh whole chicken[4, 6].......................		1.9		1.42	L-Aug.2014	3.3
Fresh and frozen chicken parts[4, 6].............		-0.4		0.72	L-Nov.2014	1.6
Other poultry including turkey[5]..................	0.066	-0.8	-0.001	0.78	L-Nov.2014	1.4
Fish and seafood[4]...................................	0.291	-0.5	-0.001	0.54	S-Oct.2014	-0.5
Fresh fish and seafood[5]...........................	0.148	0.0	0.000	0.87	L-Nov.2014	0.1
Processed fish and seafood[5].......................	0.142	-0.8	-0.001	0.53	S-Nov.2013	-1.2

See footnotes at end of table.

Expenditure category	Relative importance Dec. 2014	One Month			Largest (L) or Smallest (S) seasonally adjusted change since:[3]	
		Seasonally adjusted percent change Dec. 2014-Jan. 2015	Seasonally adjusted effect on All Items Dec. 2014-Jan. 2015[1]	Standard error, median price change[2]	Date	Percent change
Shelf stable fish and seafood[4, 6]		-0.3		0.88	L-Nov.2014	0.9
Frozen fish and seafood[6]		-1.0		0.75	S-Nov.2013	-1.2
Eggs	0.134	-1.8	-0.002	0.62	S-Sep.2012	-2.9
Dairy and related products[4]	0.898	-0.9	-0.008	0.26	S-Apr.2012	-1.0
Milk[4, 5]	0.283	-2.2	-0.006	0.33	S-Mar.2009	-4.4
Fresh whole milk[4, 6]		-1.5		0.53	S-May 2013	-1.7
Fresh milk other than whole[4, 5, 6]		-2.5		0.45	S-Mar.2009	-3.2
Cheese and related products	0.286	-1.5	-0.004	0.46	S-Jul.2012	-1.5
Ice cream and related products	0.126	-1.3	-0.002	0.83	S-Jun.2012	-1.7
Other dairy and related products[4, 5]	0.204	-0.1	0.000	0.57	S-Nov.2014	-0.4
Fruits and vegetables	1.379	-0.9	-0.012	0.37	S-Dec.2013	-1.2
Fresh fruits and vegetables	1.076	-1.1	-0.012	0.46	S-Dec.2013	-1.6
Fresh fruits	0.575	-0.9	-0.005	0.64	L-Oct.2014	1.4
Apples	0.083	1.2	0.001	1.11	L-Jun.2014	1.7
Bananas	0.087	-1.2	-0.001	0.62	L-Nov.2014	1.5
Citrus fruits[5]	0.146	-0.9	-0.001	1.44	–	–
Oranges, including tangerines[6]		1.0		1.41	L-Oct.2014	2.3
Other fresh fruits[5]	0.259	-2.0	-0.005	1.08	S-Nov.2014	-3.1
Fresh vegetables	0.500	-1.4	-0.007	0.59	S-Mar.2014	-1.4
Potatoes	0.075	1.5	0.001	1.14	L-Oct.2014	2.0
Lettuce	0.072	5.0	0.003	1.44	L-Jun.2014	6.3
Tomatoes[4]	0.102	-4.4	-0.004	1.42	S-Feb.2013	-4.7
Other fresh vegetables	0.251	-2.8	-0.007	0.74	S-Feb.2012	-3.3
Processed fruits and vegetables[5]	0.303	-0.2	0.000	0.49	S-Nov.2014	-0.3
Canned fruits and vegetables[5]	0.157	0.0	0.000	0.76	S-Nov.2014	-0.7
Canned fruits[5, 6]		0.6		0.86	S-Nov.2014	-0.5
Canned vegetables[5, 6]		-0.2		1.02	S-Nov.2014	-1.2
Frozen fruits and vegetables[5]	0.088	-0.9	-0.001	0.86	S-Aug.2014	-1.8
Frozen vegetables[6]		-0.2		1.07	S-Nov.2014	-1.0
Other processed fruits and vegetables including dried[5]	0.057	1.0	0.001	0.73	L-Jul.2013	1.3
Dried beans, peas, and lentils[4, 5, 6]		-1.3		0.79	S-Apr.2013	-2.1
Nonalcoholic beverages and beverage materials	0.955	0.1	0.001	0.34	L-Nov.2014	0.5
Juices and nonalcoholic drinks[5]	0.699	-0.3	-0.002	0.43	L-Nov.2014	0.5
Carbonated drinks	0.285	-1.1	-0.003	0.68	S-May 2013	-1.3
Frozen noncarbonated juices and drinks[4, 5]	0.014	0.2	0.000	0.64	L-Nov.2014	0.6
Nonfrozen noncarbonated juices and drinks[5]	0.400	0.0	0.000	0.61	L-Nov.2014	1.0
Beverage materials including coffee and tea[5]	0.256	0.7	0.002	0.44	L-Jul.2014	0.7
Coffee	0.158	1.4	0.002	0.59	L-Aug.2014	1.7
Roasted coffee[6]		2.0		0.64	L-May 2011	2.1
Instant and freeze dried coffee[4, 6]		-0.1		1.03	S-Nov.2014	-0.8
Other beverage materials including tea[5]	0.099	-1.1	-0.001	0.62	S-Nov.2013	-1.3
Other food at home	2.043	-0.1	-0.003	0.23	S-Oct.2014	-0.3
Sugar and sweets[4]	0.299	1.9	0.006	0.58	L-Jan.2009	2.1
Sugar and artificial sweeteners	0.054	2.1	0.001	0.62	L-Apr.2008	2.6
Candy and chewing gum[4, 5]	0.185	0.9	0.002	0.89	L-Sep.2014	2.1
Other sweets[5]	0.060	0.4	0.000	0.63	L-Nov.2014	1.0
Fats and oils	0.245	-0.6	-0.001	0.42	S-Nov.2014	-0.8
Butter and margarine[5]	0.077	-1.5	-0.001	0.65	S-Dec.2010	-1.6
Butter[6]		-2.5		0.92	S-Mar.2012	-2.8
Margarine[6]		-2.6		1.02	S-May 2005	-3.1
Salad dressing[5]	0.062	0.6	0.000	0.82	L-Feb.2014	1.0
Other fats and oils including peanut butter[5]	0.107	-0.5	0.000	0.62	S-Nov.2014	-0.5

See footnotes at end of table.

Expenditure category	Relative importance Dec. 2014	Seasonally adjusted percent change Dec. 2014-Jan. 2015	Seasonally adjusted effect on All Items Dec. 2014-Jan. 2015[1]	Standard error, median price change[2]	Largest (L) or Smallest (S) seasonally adjusted change since:[3]	
					Date	Percent change
Peanut butter[4, 5, 6]		-1.3		1.00	S-Jul.2014	-1.9
Other foods	1.499	-0.5	-0.007	0.28	S-Aug.2013	-1.0
Soups	0.093	-0.6	-0.001	1.02	S-Oct.2014	-0.8
Frozen and freeze dried prepared foods[4]	0.285	-1.4	-0.004	0.63	S-Jan.2014	-1.8
Snacks[4]	0.330	-0.7	-0.002	0.66	S-Jun.2014	-0.7
Spices, seasonings, condiments, sauces	0.292	-0.4	-0.001	0.59	S-Oct.2014	-0.6
Salt and other seasonings and spices[5, 6]		-1.3		0.93	S-Jan.2010	-1.7
Olives, pickles, relishes[4, 5, 6]		0.1		1.56	S-Nov.2014	-2.2
Sauces and gravies[5, 6]		1.3		0.87	L-May 2014	2.7
Other condiments[6]		-0.6		0.97	S-Sep.2014	-1.2
Baby food[4, 5]	0.055	-0.2	0.000	0.38	S-Sep.2014	-0.2
Other miscellaneous foods[4, 5]	0.444	-0.9	-0.004	0.51	S-Aug.2014	-1.0
Prepared salads[4, 7, 6]		-0.8		0.55	S-Oct.2014	-0.9
Food away from home[4]	5.830	0.2	0.009	0.06	S-Oct.2014	0.2
Full service meals and snacks[4, 5]	2.823	0.1	0.003	0.07	S-Apr.2014	0.1
Limited service meals and snacks[4, 5]	2.413	0.3	0.006	0.10	–	–
Food at employee sites and schools[5]	0.212	0.1	0.000	0.16	–	–
Food at elementary and secondary schools[8, 6]		0.1		0.08	L-Nov.2014	0.2
Food from vending machines and mobile vendors[4, 5]	0.064	0.8	0.000	0.34	L-Nov.2012	1.0
Other food away from home[4, 5]	0.319	0.0	0.000	0.11	S-Oct.2014	-0.1
Energy	8.030	-9.7	-0.812	0.15	S-Nov.2008	-18.0
Energy commodities	4.215	-18.0	-0.808	0.12	S-Dec.2008	-18.5
Fuel oil and other fuels[4]	0.236	-7.1	-0.017	0.53	S-Mar.2014	-7.2
Fuel oil[4]	0.139	-9.9	-0.014	0.37	S-Dec.2008	-12.6
Propane, kerosene, and firewood[4, 9]	0.097	-7.7	-0.007	0.78	S-Mar.2014	-12.1
Motor fuel	3.979	-18.6	-0.791	0.12	S-Dec.2008	-19.2
Gasoline (all types)	3.904	-18.7	-0.783	0.12	S-Dec.2008	-19.5
Gasoline, unleaded regular[6]		-19.1		0.38	S-Dec.2008	-19.9
Gasoline, unleaded midgrade[10, 6]		-18.1		0.36	S-Dec.2008	-18.6
Gasoline, unleaded premium[6]		-16.4		0.31	S-Dec.2008	-18.3
Other motor fuels[5]	0.075	-13.5	-0.010	0.12	S-Dec.2008	-13.7
Energy services[11]	3.815	-0.1	-0.004	0.28	S-Nov.2014	-0.3
Electricity[11]	2.940	0.9	0.026	0.35	L-May 2014	2.0
Utility (piped) gas service[11]	0.875	-3.4	-0.030	0.28	S-Nov.2010	-3.5
All items less food and energy	77.713	0.2	0.138	0.04	L-Oct.2014	0.2
Commodities less food and energy commodities	19.408	-0.1	-0.023	0.09	L-Oct.2014	0.0
Household furnishings and supplies[12]	3.342	-0.3	-0.010	0.16	–	–
Window and floor coverings and other linens[4, 5]	0.266	1.1	0.003	0.56	L-Jan.2014	1.5
Floor coverings[4, 5]	0.047	0.8	0.000	0.41	L-Aug.2014	0.8
Window coverings[4, 5]	0.053	-1.7	-0.001	0.50	L-Nov.2014	3.4
Other linens[4, 5]	0.166	2.0	0.003	0.83	L-Jan.2014	2.2
Furniture and bedding[4]	0.769	-0.5	-0.004	0.31	S-Sep.2014	-0.7
Bedroom furniture[4]	0.268	-1.4	-0.004	0.47	S-Jul.2014	-1.4
Living room, kitchen, and dining room furniture[4, 5]	0.363	0.1	0.000	0.50	S-Sep.2014	-0.7
Other furniture[5]	0.128	-0.2	0.000	0.61	S-Nov.2014	-0.7
Infants' furniture[4, 8, 6]						
Appliances[5]	0.271	0.1	0.000	0.46	L-Jul.2014	0.3
Major appliances[5]	0.147	-0.4	-0.001	0.67	S-Nov.2014	-1.8
Laundry equipment[6]		0.0		0.95	S-Nov.2014	-3.7
Other appliances[4, 5]	0.120	1.0	0.001	0.66	L-Mar.2014	1.2
Other household equipment and furnishings[5]	0.479	-0.3	-0.001	0.51	L-Oct.2014	0.4
Clocks, lamps, and decorator items[4]	0.257	0.7	0.002	0.88	L-Oct.2014	0.8

See footnotes at end of table.

Expenditure category	Relative importance Dec. 2014	One Month				
		Seasonally adjusted percent change Dec. 2014-Jan. 2015	Seasonally adjusted effect on All Items Dec. 2014-Jan. 2015[1]	Standard error, median price change[2]	Largest (L) or Smallest (S) seasonally adjusted change since:[3]	
					Date	Percent change
Indoor plants and flowers[13]	0.107	0.2	0.000	0.50	–	–
Dishes and flatware[4, 5]	0.041	3.4	0.001	1.23	L-Jun.2014	3.4
Nonelectric cookware and tableware[5]	0.074	-1.5	-0.001	0.42	S-Jul.2003	-2.1
Tools, hardware, outdoor equipment and supplies[5]	0.710	-0.6	-0.004	0.25	S-Apr.2014	-0.8
Tools, hardware and supplies[4, 5]	0.189	0.0	0.000	0.39	S-Nov.2014	-0.5
Outdoor equipment and supplies[5]	0.367	-0.8	-0.003	0.32	S-Nov.2013	-0.8
Housekeeping supplies[4]	0.847	-0.4	-0.003	0.26	S-Jul.2014	-0.5
Household cleaning products[5]	0.337	-0.7	-0.002	0.45	S-May 2010	-1.2
Household paper products[4, 5]	0.247	-0.6	-0.001	0.43	S-Nov.2014	-0.6
Miscellaneous household products[4, 5]	0.263	0.4	0.001	0.41	L-Oct.2014	0.8
Apparel	3.343	0.3	0.009	0.41	L-Jun.2014	0.3
Men's and boys' apparel	0.834	0.1	0.001	0.74	L-Sep.2014	0.4
Men's apparel	0.653	-0.5	-0.003	0.80	L-Nov.2014	-0.1
Men's suits, sport coats, and outerwear	0.104	1.2	0.001	2.00	L-Sep.2014	1.2
Men's furnishings	0.185	-2.5	-0.005	0.89	S-Feb.1994	-2.9
Men's shirts and sweaters[5]	0.196	-1.5	-0.003	1.56	S-Aug.2014	-2.9
Men's pants and shorts	0.160	1.4	0.002	1.57	L-Feb.2014	1.9
Boys' apparel	0.181	2.1	0.004	1.48	L-Apr.2014	2.3
Women's and girls' apparel	1.439	0.8	0.011	0.73	L-Dec.2013	1.7
Women's apparel	1.210	0.0	0.000	0.78	L-Aug.2014	0.3
Women's outerwear	0.118	3.3	0.004	2.43	L-Jun.2014	6.3
Women's dresses	0.155	-2.6	-0.004	2.38	S-Apr.2014	-2.6
Women's suits and separates[5]	0.550	-1.2	-0.007	0.97	S-Nov.2014	-1.6
Women's underwear, nightwear, sportswear and accessories[5]	0.378	0.0	0.000	0.92	L-Oct.2014	0.1
Girls' apparel	0.229	4.9	0.011	1.83	L-Oct.2012	5.1
Footwear	0.725	-0.7	-0.005	0.73	S-Jul.2013	-0.7
Men's footwear[4]	0.218	0.2	0.001	1.07	L-Sep.2014	0.9
Boys' and girls' footwear	0.178	-1.8	-0.003	1.10	S-Nov.2010	-3.1
Women's footwear	0.329	-0.9	-0.003	1.17	S-Jun.2014	-1.6
Infants' and toddlers' apparel	0.135	0.0	0.000	0.98	–	–
Jewelry and watches[9]	0.211	0.7	0.001	0.78	L-Dec.2012	0.7
Watches[4, 9]	0.046	2.6	0.001	0.87	L-Sep.2013	5.0
Jewelry[9]	0.164	0.1	0.000	0.96	L-Sep.2014	0.4
Transportation commodities less motor fuel[12]	5.685	-0.1	-0.006	0.09	L-Oct.2014	-0.1
New vehicles	3.551	-0.1	-0.005	0.14	S-Jun.2014	-0.3
New cars and trucks[5, 6]		-0.1		0.12	S-Jun.2014	-0.3
New cars[6]		-0.1		0.14	–	–
New trucks[14, 6]		-0.4		0.13	S-Aug.2009	-0.8
Used cars and trucks	1.591	-0.1	-0.002	0.01	L-Sep.2014	0.0
Motor vehicle parts and equipment[4]	0.435	0.2	0.001	0.21	S-Nov.2014	-0.2
Tires[4]	0.285	0.3	0.001	0.29	S-Nov.2014	-0.4
Vehicle accessories other than tires[4, 5]	0.150	-0.1	0.000	0.27	S-Sep.2014	-0.1
Vehicle parts and equipment other than tires[4, 6]		-0.3		0.24	S-May 2014	-0.5
Motor oil, coolant, and fluids[4, 6]		-0.3		0.52	S-Nov.2014	-0.5
Medical care commodities	1.772	-0.3	-0.005	0.21	S-Dec.2013	-0.7
Medicinal drugs[4, 12]	1.696	0.1	0.002	0.22	S-Oct.2014	0.0
Prescription drugs	1.345	-0.2	-0.002	0.24	S-Mar.2014	-0.2
Nonprescription drugs[4, 12]	0.351	-1.0	-0.003	0.47	S-Oct.2014	-2.1
Medical equipment and supplies[4, 12]	0.076	-1.5	-0.001	0.39	S-Jul.2011	-2.0
Recreation commodities[12]	2.007	-0.5	-0.010	0.17	S-Nov.2014	-0.6
Video and audio products[12]	0.289	-0.4	-0.001	0.35	L-Apr.2014	-0.4

See footnotes at end of table.

Expenditure category	Relative importance Dec. 2014	One Month				
		Seasonally adjusted percent change Dec. 2014- Jan. 2015	Seasonally adjusted effect on All Items Dec. 2014- Jan. 2015[1]	Standard error, median price change[2]	Largest (L) or Smallest (S) seasonally adjusted change since:[3]	
					Date	Percent change
Televisions...	0.133	-0.9	-0.001	0.60	L-Aug.2014	-0.7
Other video equipment[4, 5].............................	0.029	2.0	0.001	0.78	L-Apr.2014	3.6
Audio equipment..	0.066	-1.0	-0.001	0.55	S-Nov.2014	-1.2
Audio discs, tapes and other media[4, 5]...............	0.044	0.4	0.000	0.62	S-Nov.2014	-0.1
Pets and pet products[4].................................	0.659	-0.8	-0.005	0.30	S-Jul.2014	-0.9
Pet food[4, 5, 6]..		-1.1		0.33	S-EVER	–
Purchase of pets, pet supplies, accessories[4, 5, 6]....		-0.6		0.43	S-Aug.2014	-0.9
Sporting goods[4]..	0.400	0.1	0.000	0.31	L-Sep.2014	0.4
Sports vehicles including bicycles[4]...................	0.181	0.6	0.001	0.43	L-Apr.2014	0.8
Sports equipment.......................................	0.214	-0.2	0.000	0.44	L-Oct.2014	-0.2
Photographic equipment and supplies..................	0.058	-1.8	-0.001	0.96	S-Jul.2013	-1.8
Film and photographic supplies[4, 5, 6]..................		-0.2		0.64	L-Nov.2014	0.9
Photographic equipment[5, 6]............................		-1.7		1.06	S-Feb.2014	-3.1
Recreational reading materials[4]........................	0.220	0.1	0.000	0.48	–	–
Newspapers and magazines[4, 5]........................	0.123	-0.4	0.000	0.68	S-Nov.2014	-0.4
Recreational books[4, 5].................................	0.094	0.7	0.001	0.59	L-Oct.2014	0.8
Other recreational goods[5].............................	0.381	-0.9	-0.003	0.48	S-Apr.2014	-1.2
Toys...	0.277	-0.8	-0.002	0.59	S-Nov.2014	-0.8
Toys, games, hobbies and playground equipment[5, 6]..		-0.2		0.68	S-Nov.2014	-0.2
Sewing machines, fabric and supplies[4, 5]............	0.050	-1.2	-0.001	1.32	L-Nov.2014	0.0
Music instruments and accessories[5]..................	0.042	-1.2	-0.001	0.42	S-Nov.2013	-1.2
Education and communication commodities[12]............	0.610	-0.5	-0.003	0.30	L-Oct.2014	-0.2
Educational books and supplies........................	0.203	0.3	0.001	0.45	S-Nov.2014	0.3
College textbooks[4, 15, 6]................................		0.8		0.41	L-Sep.2014	1.0
Information technology commodities[12]..................	0.408	-0.9	-0.004	0.40	L-Oct.2014	-0.6
Personal computers and peripheral equipment[7].....	0.272	-1.3	-0.003	0.49	L-Nov.2014	-1.3
Computer software and accessories[4, 5]..............	0.068	-0.6	0.000	0.82	L-Nov.2014	0.4
Telephone hardware, calculators, and other consumer information items[4, 5]......................	0.068	0.1	0.000	0.84	L-Aug.2014	0.2
Alcoholic beverages......................................	1.015	-0.3	-0.003	0.16	–	–
Alcoholic beverages at home...........................	0.597	-0.6	-0.004	0.23	S-Jan.2010	-0.6
Beer, ale, and other malt beverages at home........	0.274	-0.4	-0.001	0.28	S-May 2011	-0.5
Distilled spirits at home[4]..............................	0.073	-0.4	0.000	0.39	S-Jun.2014	-0.8
Whiskey at home[4, 6]..................................		0.7		0.40	L-Mar.2014	1.2
Distilled spirits, excluding whiskey, at home[6]......		-0.7		0.55	S-Jun.2014	-0.7
Wine at home..	0.250	-0.7	-0.002	0.44	S-Oct.2013	-0.8
Alcoholic beverages away from home[4].................	0.418	0.0	0.000	0.18	–	–
Beer, ale, and other malt beverages away from home[4, 5, 6]..		-0.1		0.15	–	–
Wine away from home[4, 5, 6]...........................		0.0		0.24	–	–
Distilled spirits away from home[4, 5, 6].................		0.0		0.20	–	–
Other goods[12]...	1.634	0.4	0.007	0.18	L-Jun.2014	0.4
Tobacco and smoking products.........................	0.718	-0.2	-0.002	0.16	S-Jul.2014	-0.9
Cigarettes[5]...	0.661	-0.1	-0.001	0.17	S-Jul.2014	-1.0
Tobacco products other than cigarettes[4, 5]..........	0.050	-1.2	-0.001	0.53	S-Nov.2006	-1.4
Personal care products[4]...............................	0.724	1.2	0.009	0.31	L-Mar.2013	1.2
Hair, dental, shaving, and miscellaneous personal care products[4, 5]......................................	0.369	1.2	0.004	0.46	L-Mar.2013	1.2
Cosmetics, perfume, bath, nail preparations and implements[4]...	0.348	1.2	0.004	0.40	L-Dec.2013	1.2
Miscellaneous personal goods[5].........................	0.192	-0.2	0.000	0.44	S-Nov.2014	-1.3
Stationery, stationery supplies, gift wrap[6].............		-0.9		0.54	S-Nov.2014	-1.1

See footnotes at end of table.

Expenditure category	Relative importance Dec. 2014	One Month				
		Seasonally adjusted percent change Dec. 2014- Jan. 2015	Seasonally adjusted effect on All Items Dec. 2014- Jan. 2015[1]	Standard error, median price change[2]	Largest (L) or Smallest (S) seasonally adjusted change since:[3]	
					Date	Percent change
Infants' equipment[4, 8, 6]		-1.9		0.51	S-Aug.2011	-2.3
Services less energy services	58.305	0.3	0.158	0.04	L-May 2014	0.3
Shelter	32.711	0.3	0.088	0.06	L-Sep.2014	0.3
Rent of shelter[16]	32.336	0.3	0.082	0.06	L-Oct.2014	0.3
Rent of primary residence[11]	7.159	0.2	0.018	0.04	–	–
Lodging away from home[5]	0.839	1.3	0.011	1.89	L-May 2014	1.9
Housing at school, excluding board[11, 16]	0.172	0.3	0.001	0.04	–	–
Other lodging away from home including hotels and motels	0.666	1.5	0.011	2.30	L-May 2014	2.3
Owners' equivalent rent of residences[11, 16]	24.339	0.2	0.057	0.03	–	–
Owners' equivalent rent of primary residence[11, 16]	22.918	0.2	0.053	0.03	–	–
Tenants' and household insurance[4, 5]	0.375	0.7	0.002	0.31	S-Nov.2014	0.1
Water and sewer and trash collection services[5]	1.222	0.1	0.002	0.13	S-Aug.2013	0.1
Water and sewerage maintenance[11]	0.945	0.2	0.002	0.16	S-May 2014	0.2
Garbage and trash collection[4, 14]	0.277	-0.1	0.000	0.17	S-Apr.2012	-0.2
Household operations[4, 5]	0.848	0.2	0.002	0.14	L-Oct.2014	0.8
Domestic services[4, 5]	0.279	0.3	0.001	0.12	L-Oct.2014	0.4
Gardening and lawncare services[4, 5]	0.279	-0.2	-0.001	0.09	S-May 2013	-0.2
Moving, storage, freight expense[5]	0.116	1.1	0.001	0.59	L-Dec.2012	1.6
Repair of household items[4, 5]	0.066	0.3	0.000	0.12	S-Nov.2014	0.1
Medical care services	5.944	0.1	0.005	0.08	S-Sep.2014	0.1
Professional services	3.032	0.0	0.001	0.10	S-Jul.2014	0.0
Physicians' services[11]	1.590	0.1	0.001	0.13	S-Oct.2014	0.1
Dental services[11]	0.804	0.5	0.004	0.11	L-Mar.2013	0.5
Eyeglasses and eye care[4, 9]	0.284	-0.8	-0.002	0.38	S-May 2011	-0.9
Services by other medical professionals[11, 9]	0.354	-0.8	-0.003	0.14	S-Jul.1995	-0.9
Hospital and related services	2.159	0.2	0.004	0.11	S-Sep.2014	0.2
Hospital services[11, 17]	1.853	0.2	0.003	0.12	S-Sep.2014	0.2
Inpatient hospital services[11, 17, 6]		-0.1		0.21	S-Nov.2013	-0.2
Outpatient hospital services[11, 9, 6]		0.4		0.20	S-Nov.2014	0.1
Nursing homes and adult day services[11, 17]	0.174	0.3	0.001	0.10	L-Nov.2014	0.3
Care of invalids and elderly at home[4, 8]	0.132	0.2	0.000	0.10	S-Nov.2014	0.1
Health insurance[4, 8]	0.753	0.2	0.001	0.08	L-Feb.2014	0.4
Transportation services	5.625	0.4	0.021	0.14	L-Oct.2014	0.5
Leased cars and trucks[15]	0.397	0.7	0.003	0.31	L-Dec.2012	0.8
Car and truck rental[5]	0.073	3.7	0.003	1.50	L-Dec.2013	3.7
Motor vehicle maintenance and repair[4]	1.168	0.1	0.001	0.17	–	–
Motor vehicle body work[4]	0.057	0.2	0.000	0.14	S-Nov.2014	0.1
Motor vehicle maintenance and servicing[4]	0.492	-0.2	-0.001	0.20	S-May 2014	-0.3
Motor vehicle repair[4, 5]	0.587	0.4	0.002	0.27	L-Oct.2014	0.5
Motor vehicle insurance	2.300	0.6	0.015	0.23	L-Apr.2014	0.8
Motor vehicle fees[4, 5]	0.565	0.1	0.001	0.11	–	–
State motor vehicle registration and license fees[4, 11, 5]	0.312	0.1	0.000	0.08	L-Oct.2014	0.2
Parking and other fees[5]	0.235	-0.5	-0.001	0.18	S-EVER	–
Parking fees and tolls[4, 5, 6]		0.2		0.24	S-Oct.2014	0.1
Automobile service clubs[4, 5, 6]		0.5		0.17	L-Oct.2014	1.1
Public transportation	1.122	-0.1	-0.001	0.36	L-Nov.2014	0.0
Airline fare	0.702	-0.3	-0.002	0.51	L-Nov.2014	-0.2
Other intercity transportation	0.157	-0.9	-0.001	0.67	S-Apr.2011	-0.9
Intercity bus fare[4, 7, 6]						
Intercity train fare[4, 7, 6]		-6.2		1.12	S-Sep.2014	-6.6

See footnotes at end of table.

Table 6. Consumer Price Index for All Urban Consumers (CPI-U): U.S. city average, by expenditure category, January 2015, 1-month analysis table — Continued

[1982-84=100, unless otherwise noted]

Expenditure category	Relative importance Dec. 2014	One Month Seasonally adjusted percent change Dec. 2014-Jan. 2015	Seasonally adjusted effect on All Items Dec. 2014-Jan. 2015[1]	Standard error, median price change[2]	Largest (L) or Smallest (S) seasonally adjusted change since:[3] Date	Percent change
Ship fare[4, 5, 6]		0.4		0.79	L-Nov.2014	2.2
Intracity transportation[4]	0.260	0.3	0.001	0.06	L-Sep.2014	0.5
Intracity mass transit[4, 12, 6]		0.1		0.08	L-Oct.2014	0.1
Recreation services[12]	3.744	0.5	0.019	0.16	L-Jun.2012	0.7
Video and audio services[12]	1.558	0.1	0.002	0.13	S-Nov.2014	-0.1
Cable and satellite television and radio service[14]	1.468	0.1	0.001	0.13	S-Nov.2014	-0.1
Video discs and other media, including rental of video and audio[4, 5]	0.090	1.4	0.001	0.90	L-Oct.2014	1.5
Video discs and other media[4, 5, 6]		1.7		1.27	L-Oct.2014	2.0
Rental of video or audio discs and other media[4, 5, 6]		1.2		0.29	–	–
Pet services including veterinary[5]	0.399	0.6	0.002	0.11	L-Feb.2011	0.9
Pet services[4, 5, 6]		0.3		0.12	L-Jun.2014	0.4
Veterinarian services[5, 6]		0.6		0.12	L-Jul.2012	0.7
Photographers and film processing[4, 5]	0.062	0.1	0.000	0.39	S-Nov.2014	-0.1
Photographer fees[4, 5, 6]		0.0		0.14	S-Nov.2014	-1.3
Film processing[4, 5, 6]		0.7		0.57	L-Apr.2014	0.9
Other recreation services[5]	1.724	0.8	0.014	0.33	L-Jun.2012	1.1
Club dues and fees for participant sports and group exercises[5]	0.602	1.4	0.008	0.45	L-Sep.2013	1.4
Admissions[4]	0.640	0.6	0.004	0.55	S-Nov.2014	0.0
Admission to movies, theaters, and concerts[4, 5, 6]		0.1		0.52	S-Nov.2014	-0.4
Admission to sporting events[4, 5, 6]		1.8		0.66	L-Jan.2012	3.0
Fees for lessons or instructions[4, 9]	0.211	0.1	0.000	0.18	L-Oct.2014	0.4
Education and communication services[12]	6.452	0.2	0.015	0.07	L-Jun.2014	0.3
Tuition, other school fees, and childcare	3.122	0.5	0.015	0.08	L-Oct.2014	0.5
College tuition and fees	1.853	0.4	0.007	0.12	L-Oct.2014	0.7
Elementary and high school tuition and fees	0.377	0.3	0.001	0.07	–	–
Child care and nursery school[13]	0.725	0.5	0.003	0.11	L-Mar.2014	0.5
Technical and business school tuition and fees[5]	0.039	0.2	0.000	0.10	–	–
Postage and delivery services[5]	0.144	-0.5	-0.001	0.02	S-Feb.2011	-1.1
Postage[4]	0.130	-0.5	-0.001	0.00	S-Feb.2011	-1.3
Delivery services[5]	0.014	0.1	0.000	0.18	L-Aug.2014	0.2
Telephone services[4, 5]	2.462	0.0	-0.001	0.10	L-Sep.2014	0.0
Wireless telephone services[4, 5]	1.624	-0.5	-0.008	0.12	–	–
Land-line telephone services[4, 12]	0.837	0.8	0.007	0.13	L-Jan.2014	1.6
Internet services and electronic information providers[5]	0.711	0.2	0.001	0.26	L-Oct.2014	0.4
Other personal services[4, 12]	1.760	0.4	0.007	0.08	L-Feb.2013	0.5
Personal care services[4]	0.638	-0.1	-0.001	0.11	S-Oct.2013	-0.3
Haircuts and other personal care services[4, 5]	0.638	-0.1	-0.001	0.11	S-Oct.2013	-0.3
Miscellaneous personal services	1.122	0.6	0.007	0.10	L-Oct.2009	0.7
Legal services[9]	0.316	0.2	0.001	0.15	L-Jun.2014	0.4
Funeral expenses[4, 9]	0.173	0.3	0.000	0.12	L-Oct.2014	0.3
Laundry and dry cleaning services[4, 5]	0.276	0.2	0.001	0.11	L-Nov.2014	0.2
Apparel services other than laundry and dry cleaning[4, 5]	0.034	0.4	0.000	0.17	L-Oct.2014	0.7
Financial services[4, 9]	0.228	2.2	0.005	0.28	L-Sep.2008	3.0
Checking account and other bank services[4, 5, 6]		0.1		0.02	S-Nov.2014	0.0
Tax return preparation and other accounting fees[5, 6]		3.2		0.39	L-Sep.2008	3.4

See footnotes at end of table.

Table 6. Consumer Price Index for All Urban Consumers (CPI-U): U.S. city average, by expenditure category, January 2015, 1-month analysis table — Continued

[1982-84=100, unless otherwise noted]

Expenditure category	Relative importance Dec. 2014	One Month				
		Seasonally adjusted percent change Dec. 2014-Jan. 2015	Seasonally adjusted effect on All Items Dec. 2014-Jan. 2015[1]	Standard error, median price change[2]	Largest (L) or Smallest (S) seasonally adjusted change since:[3]	
					Date	Percent change
Special aggregate indexes						
All items less food.........................	85.743	-0.8	-0.674	0.04	S-Dec.2008	-1.0
All items less shelter........................	67.289	-1.1	-0.769	0.04	S-Dec.2008	-1.2
All items less food and shelter.................	53.032	-1.4	-0.763	0.05	S-Dec.2008	-1.6
All items less food, shelter, and energy........	45.002	0.1	0.049	0.05	L-Oct.2014	0.1
All items less food, shelter, energy, and used cars and trucks.......................	43.411	0.1	0.051	0.05	L-Oct.2014	0.2
All items less medical care....................	92.284	-0.7	-0.680	0.04	S-Dec.2008	-0.9
All items less energy........................	91.970	0.1	0.131	0.03	–	–
Commodities...............................	37.880	-2.2	-0.835	0.06	S-Nov.2008	-4.4
Commodities less food, energy, and used cars and trucks..............................	17.817	-0.1	-0.020	0.10	L-Oct.2014	0.1
Commodities less food.......................	23.623	-3.5	-0.829	0.07	S-Nov.2008	-6.7
Commodities less food and beverages..........	22.608	-3.6	-0.827	0.08	S-Nov.2008	-7.1
Services..................................	62.120	0.2	0.154	0.05	–	–
Services less rent of shelter[16]................	29.784	0.1	0.042	0.07	S-Nov.2014	0.1
Services less medical care services............	56.176	0.2	0.113	0.05	–	–
Durables.................................	8.950	-0.2	-0.018	0.08	L-Oct.2014	0.0
Nondurables..............................	28.930	-2.9	-0.838	0.07	S-Nov.2008	-5.3
Nondurables less food.......................	14.673	-5.6	-0.842	0.11	S-Nov.2008	-10.2
Nondurables less food and beverages..........	13.658	-6.0	-0.840	0.11	S-Nov.2008	-11.0
Nondurables less food, beverages, and apparel.....	10.315	-7.9	-0.847	0.08	S-Nov.2008	-14.5
Nondurables less food and apparel............	11.330	-7.2	-0.848	0.07	S-Nov.2008	-13.2
Housing..................................	42.173	0.1	0.062	0.06	S-Nov.2014	0.1
Education and communication[5]...............	7.062	0.2	0.012	0.07	L-Jun.2014	0.2
Education[5]................................	3.325	0.5	0.016	0.08	L-Oct.2014	0.5
Communication[5]...........................	3.737	-0.1	-0.004	0.10	L-Sep.2014	-0.1
Information and information processing[5]........	3.593	-0.1	-0.004	0.10	L-Sep.2014	-0.1
Information technology, hardware and services[18].....	1.132	-1.1	-0.013	0.23	S-Aug.2012	-1.1
Recreation[5]..............................	5.750	0.2	0.009	0.12	L-Oct.2014	0.2
Video and audio[5]..........................	1.847	-0.4	-0.008	0.14	S-Nov.2014	-0.5
Pets, pet products and services[5].............	1.058	-0.3	-0.003	0.20	S-Jul.2014	-0.5
Photography[5].............................	0.120	-0.8	-0.001	0.54	S-Feb.2014	-0.8
Food and beverages........................	15.272	-0.1	-0.009	0.07	S-May 2013	-0.1
Domestically produced farm food..............	7.094	-0.4	-0.027	0.13	S-Sep.2009	-0.4
Other services............................	11.955	0.3	0.040	0.07	L-Jan.2014	0.3
Apparel less footwear.......................	2.619	0.5	0.014	0.48	L-Dec.2013	1.0
Fuels and utilities..........................	5.273	-0.4	-0.019	0.21	S-Apr.2014	-1.9
Household energy..........................	4.051	-0.5	-0.021	0.27	S-Apr.2014	-2.5
Medical care..............................	7.716	0.0	0.000	0.08	S-Dec.2013	0.0
Transportation............................	15.289	-5.0	-0.777	0.06	S-Dec.2008	-5.0
Private transportation.......................	14.167	-5.4	-0.776	0.07	S-Nov.2008	-10.8
New and used motor vehicles[5]...............	5.720	0.0	-0.002	0.10	L-Oct.2014	0.0
Utilities and public transportation..............	10.089	0.0	0.003	0.13	S-Nov.2014	-0.1
Household furnishings and operations..........	4.189	-0.2	-0.007	0.13	L-Oct.2014	0.4
Other goods and services....................	3.394	0.4	0.014	0.09	L-Oct.2014	0.4
Personal care.............................	2.676	0.6	0.016	0.11	L-EVER	–

[1] The 'effect' of an item category is a measure of that item's contribution to the All items price change. For example, if the Food index had an effect of 0.40, and the All items index rose 1.2 percent, then the increase in food prices contributed 0.40 / 1.2, or 33.3 percent, to that All items increase. Said another way, had food prices been unchanged for that month the change in the All items index would have been 1.2 percent minus 0.40, or 0.8 percent. Effects can be negative as well. For example, if the effect of food was a negative 0.1, and the All items index rose 0.5 percent, the All items index actually would have been 0.1 percent higher (or 0.6 percent) had food prices been unchanged. Since food prices fell while prices overall were rising, the contribution of food to the All items price change was negative (in this case, -0.1 / 0.5, or minus 20 percent).

[2] A statistic's margin of error is often expressed as its point estimate plus or minus two standard errors. For example, if a CPI category rose 0.6

percent, and its standard error was 0.15 percent, the margin of error on this item's 1-month percent change would be 0.6 percent, plus or minus 0.3 percent.

[3] If the current seasonally adjusted 1-month percent change is greater than the previous published 1-month percent change, then this column identifies the closest prior month with a 1-month percent change as (L)arge as or (L)arger than the current 1-month change. If the current 1-month percent change is smaller than the previous published 1-month percent change, the most recent month with a change as (S)mall or (S)maller than the current month change is identified. If the current and previous published 1-month percent changes are equal, a dash will appear. Standard numerical comparisons are used. For example, 0.8% is greater than 0.6%, -0.4% is less than -0.2%, and -0.2% is less than 0.0%. Note that a (L)arger change can be a smaller decline, for example, a -0.2% change is larger than a -0.4% change, but still represents a decline in the price index. Likewise, (S)maller changes can be increases, for example, a 0.6% change is smaller than 0.8%, but still represents an increase in the price index. In this context, a -0.2% change is considered to be smaller than a 0.0% change.

[4] Not seasonally adjusted.

[5] Indexes on a December 1997=100 base.

[6] Special indexes based on a substantially smaller sample. These series do not contribute to the all items index aggregation and therefore do not have a relative importance or effect.

[7] Indexes on a December 2007=100 base.

[8] Indexes on a December 2005=100 base.

[9] Indexes on a December 1986=100 base.

[10] Indexes on a December 1993=100 base.

[11] This index series was calculated using a Laspeyres estimator. All other item stratum index series were calculated using a geometric means estimator.

[12] Indexes on a December 2009=100 base.

[13] Indexes on a December 1990=100 base.

[14] Indexes on a December 1983=100 base.

[15] Indexes on a December 2001=100 base.

[16] Indexes on a December 1982=100 base.

[17] Indexes on a December 1996=100 base.

[18] Indexes on a December 1988=100 base.

NOTE: Index applies to a month as a whole, not to any specific date.

Table 7. Consumer Price Index for All Urban Consumers (CPI-U): U.S. city average, by expenditure category, January 2015, 12-month analysis table

[1982-84=100, unless otherwise noted]

Expenditure category	Relative importance Dec. 2014	Twelve Month				
		Unadjusted percent change Jan. 2014-Jan. 2015	Unadjusted effect on All Items Jan. 2014-Jan. 2015[1]	Standard error, median price change[2]	Largest (L) or Smallest (S) unadjusted change since:[3]	
					Date	Percent change
All items...	100.000	-0.1		0.08	S-Oct.2009	-0.2
Food...	14.257	3.2	0.446	0.13	S-Nov.2014	3.2
Food at home.............................	8.427	3.3	0.271	0.18	S-Oct.2014	3.3
Cereals and bakery products....................	1.138	0.9	0.010	0.40	L-Oct.2013	0.9
Cereals and cereal products....................	0.370	0.2	0.001	0.67	L-Aug.2014	0.5
Flour and prepared flour mixes........................	0.048	0.1	0.000	0.84	L-Nov.2014	0.1
Breakfast cereal.................................	0.197	0.0	0.000	1.05	S-Sep.2014	-0.7
Rice, pasta, cornmeal.................................	0.126	0.6	0.001	1.01	L-Sep.2014	0.6
Rice[4, 5].................................		-1.4		1.28	L-Sep.2014	-0.4
Bakery products...	0.767	1.2	0.009	0.49	L-Sep.2013	2.1
Bread[4]...	0.230	1.0	0.002	0.84	S-Nov.2014	-0.4
White bread[5]...............................		0.2		1.17	S-Nov.2014	-1.5
Bread other than white[5].............................		1.2		1.26	L-Oct.2014	2.0
Fresh biscuits, rolls, muffins[4]........................	0.116	3.1	0.004	1.13	L-Oct.2013	3.3
Cakes, cupcakes, and cookies....................	0.189	1.8	0.003	1.20	L-May 2014	2.2
Cookies[5].................................		1.6		1.51	L-Aug.2014	2.7
Fresh cakes and cupcakes[5]......................		1.9		1.71	L-May 2014	2.3
Other bakery products...............................	0.233	0.1	0.000	1.03	S-Sep.2014	0.0
Fresh sweetrolls, coffeecakes, doughnuts[5]......		-0.6		1.50	S-Nov.2014	-0.7
Crackers, bread, and cracker products[5].........		-0.2		1.50	S-Apr.2014	-0.8
Frozen and refrigerated bakery products, pies, tarts, turnovers[5].................................		0.6		1.38	L-Nov.2014	0.9
Meats, poultry, fish, and eggs.............................	2.014	8.7	0.161	0.38	S-Oct.2014	8.3
Meats, poultry, and fish....................................	1.880	8.7	0.151	0.40	S-Oct.2014	8.5
Meats...	1.229	12.6	0.138	0.51	S-Oct.2014	12.5
Beef and veal...	0.582	19.0	0.093	0.70	L-Jan.2004	20.4
Uncooked ground beef.............................	0.238	21.0	0.042	0.99	L-Dec.1979	25.0
Uncooked beef roasts[4].............................	0.085	21.6	0.015	1.52	L-Dec.2003	23.5
Uncooked beef steaks[4].............................	0.207	14.9	0.027	1.31	S-Jul.2014	9.0
Uncooked other beef and veal[4]...................	0.053	22.5	0.010	1.35	S-Oct.2014	20.7
Pork...	0.372	7.4	0.026	0.81	S-Mar.2014	5.3
Bacon, breakfast sausage, and related products[4].................................	0.141	2.3	0.003	1.18	S-May 2013	1.3
Bacon and related products[5]...................		-0.1		1.27	L-Oct.2014	0.5
Breakfast sausage and related products[4, 5]...		6.2		1.72	S-Nov.2013	1.3
Ham...	0.078	11.5	0.008	1.93	S-Sep.2014	11.2
Ham, excluding canned[5]........................		12.3		1.91	S-Aug.2014	11.9
Pork chops...	0.064	8.2	0.005	1.66	S-Mar.2014	4.1
Other pork including roasts and picnics[4].........	0.089	12.3	0.010	1.74	S-Mar.2014	7.2
Other meats...	0.275	7.3	0.019	0.88	S-Nov.2014	6.5
Frankfurters[5].....................................		10.3		2.45	S-Nov.2014	6.0
Lunchmeats[4, 5].....................................		6.6		1.08	L-Apr.2009	6.7
Lamb and organ meats[5]...........................		8.0		2.53	S-Nov.2014	7.9
Lamb and mutton[4, 5]...............................		3.2		4.22	–	–
Poultry...	0.360	2.0	0.007	0.83	L-Nov.2014	2.5
Chicken[4]...	0.294	2.9	0.008	0.94	L-Nov.2014	2.9
Fresh whole chicken[5]...........................		6.1		1.98	L-Aug.2014	6.2
Fresh and frozen chicken parts[5]...............		1.4		1.18	S-Oct.2014	-1.1
Other poultry including turkey[4]...................	0.066	-1.7	-0.001	1.61	S-Jan.2010	-2.1
Fish and seafood.............................	0.291	2.2	0.006	0.84	S-Jul.2013	1.8
Fresh fish and seafood[4]...........................	0.148	3.5	0.005	1.49	S-Jul.2013	2.6
Processed fish and seafood[4]......................	0.142	0.9	0.001	0.95	S-Jul.2013	0.9
Shelf stable fish and seafood[5].................		0.2		1.25	S-Aug.2014	0.0

See footnotes at end of table.

Table 7. Consumer Price Index for All Urban Consumers (CPI-U): U.S. city average, by expenditure category, January 2015, 12-month analysis table — Continued

[1982-84=100, unless otherwise noted]

Expenditure category	Relative importance Dec. 2014	Twelve Month				
		Unadjusted percent change Jan. 2014-Jan. 2015	Unadjusted effect on All Items Jan. 2014-Jan. 2015[1]	Standard error, median price change[2]	Largest (L) or Smallest (S) unadjusted change since:[3]	
					Date	Percent change
Frozen fish and seafood[5]..........................		2.3		1.70	S-Jul.2013	0.4
Eggs..	0.134	8.2	0.010	1.09	S-Nov.2014	6.2
Dairy and related products.....................	0.898	3.8	0.033	0.42	S-Apr.2014	2.8
Milk[4]...	0.283	1.1	0.003	0.64	S-Dec.2013	0.1
Fresh whole milk[5]...........................		2.1		1.04	S-Jan.2014	2.1
Fresh milk other than whole[4, 5]...............		0.7		0.89	S-Dec.2013	0.3
Cheese and related products..................	0.286	7.8	0.021	0.81	S-Sep.2014	6.8
Ice cream and related products...............	0.126	2.0	0.002	1.18	S-Nov.2014	1.3
Other dairy and related products[4]............	0.204	3.4	0.007	0.81	S-Sep.2014	2.0
Fruits and vegetables.........................	1.379	2.3	0.031	0.60	S-Nov.2014	1.7
Fresh fruits and vegetables..................	1.076	2.9	0.030	0.73	S-Nov.2014	2.1
Fresh fruits..............................	0.575	1.7	0.010	1.01	S-Feb.2014	1.6
Apples..............................	0.083	0.6	0.001	2.01	L-Jul.2014	2.5
Bananas............................	0.087	-1.3	-0.001	0.98	S-Jul.2014	-1.6
Citrus fruits[4].........................	0.146	2.9	0.004	2.67	S-Dec.2013	2.8
Oranges, including tangerines[5]..............		2.9		2.41	S-Aug.2014	1.7
Other fresh fruits[4].....................	0.259	2.4	0.006	1.57	S-Feb.2014	0.9
Fresh vegetables........................	0.500	4.3	0.021	0.92	S-Nov.2014	0.4
Potatoes............................	0.075	-0.9	-0.001	1.93	L-Jul.2014	1.3
Lettuce.............................	0.072	12.2	0.008	2.31	L-Apr.2013	14.8
Tomatoes...........................	0.102	9.6	0.009	1.99	S-Nov.2014	7.6
Other fresh vegetables..................	0.251	1.9	0.005	1.33	S-Nov.2014	-2.2
Processed fruits and vegetables[4]...........	0.303	0.2	0.001	0.64	S-Nov.2014	-0.1
Canned fruits and vegetables[4]...........	0.157	-0.2	0.000	1.05	–	–
Canned fruits[4, 5]......................		1.1		1.33	L-Dec.2013	1.2
Canned vegetables[4, 5]..................		-0.3		1.44	S-Nov.2014	-1.0
Frozen fruits and vegetables[4]............	0.088	0.6	0.001	1.18	S-Oct.2014	0.2
Frozen vegetables[5]...................		1.0		1.47	L-Sep.2012	2.6
Other processed fruits and vegetables including dried[4]................	0.057	0.7	0.000	1.17	L-Oct.2014	0.8
Dried beans, peas, and lentils[4, 5]................		3.8		2.10	S-Oct.2014	3.1
Nonalcoholic beverages and beverage materials.........	0.955	0.9	0.009	0.45	L-Nov.2014	1.4
Juices and nonalcoholic drinks[4]............................	0.699	0.0	0.000	0.53	S-Sep.2014	-0.4
Carbonated drinks........................	0.285	0.0	0.000	0.84	S-Sep.2014	0.0
Frozen noncarbonated juices and drinks[4]............	0.014	2.3	0.000	1.20	–	–
Nonfrozen noncarbonated juices and drinks[4].........	0.400	0.0	0.000	0.83	L-Nov.2014	1.3
Beverage materials including coffee and tea[4]..........	0.256	3.5	0.009	0.78	L-Apr.2012	3.5
Coffee...................................	0.158	6.1	0.009	1.06	L-Mar.2012	9.8
Roasted coffee[5]......................		6.7		1.22	L-Mar.2012	11.0
Instant and freeze dried coffee[5]..................		2.9		1.65	L-May 2012	4.1
Other beverage materials including tea[4]..............	0.099	-0.5	0.000	0.88	S-Oct.2014	-0.6
Other food at home............................	2.043	1.3	0.026	0.34	S-Jul.2014	0.7
Sugar and sweets............................	0.299	2.0	0.006	0.76	L-Aug.2012	2.5
Sugar and artificial sweeteners.....................	0.054	0.9	0.001	1.02	L-Jul.2012	1.4
Candy and chewing gum[4]...........................	0.185	2.9	0.005	1.19	L-Aug.2012	3.0
Other sweets[4].................................	0.060	0.1	0.000	0.96	L-Nov.2014	0.3
Fats and oils...............................	0.245	0.8	0.002	0.66	S-Jun.2014	0.0
Butter and margarine[4].................................	0.077	8.8	0.006	1.16	S-Jul.2014	8.6
Butter[5]................................		19.5		1.61	S-Aug.2014	18.8
Margarine[5].............................		-0.4		1.36	S-Apr.2014	-1.7
Salad dressing[4]..............................	0.062	-2.1	-0.001	1.06	L-Jul.2014	-1.7
Other fats and oils including peanut butter[4]..........	0.107	-2.7	-0.003	1.06	S-Nov.2014	-3.1
Peanut butter[4, 5].....................................		-5.1		1.50	S-Feb.2014	-5.7
Other foods.................................	1.499	1.2	0.018	0.40	S-Jul.2014	1.2

See footnotes at end of table.

Expenditure category	Relative importance Dec. 2014	Twelve Month				
		Unadjusted percent change Jan. 2014-Jan. 2015	Unadjusted effect on All Items Jan. 2014-Jan. 2015[1]	Standard error, median price change[2]	Largest (L) or Smallest (S) unadjusted change since:[3]	
					Date	Percent change
Soups................................	0.093	-1.6	-0.002	1.38	S-Apr.2014	-2.6
Frozen and freeze dried prepared foods...........	0.285	2.3	0.006	0.91	L-Nov.2014	3.0
Snacks................................	0.330	1.0	0.003	1.07	S-Oct.2014	0.5
Spices, seasonings, condiments, sauces...........	0.292	1.9	0.005	0.90	S-Nov.2014	1.2
Salt and other seasonings and spices[4,5].......		2.4		1.35	S-Dec.2013	0.7
Olives, pickles, relishes[4,5].....................		0.4		2.00	L-Oct.2014	0.9
Sauces and gravies[4,5]............................		3.2		1.34	L-Oct.2011	4.4
Other condiments[5]..............................		1.2		1.74	S-Nov.2014	-1.7
Baby food[4]..	0.055	1.9	0.001	0.77	S-Jul.2014	1.7
Other miscellaneous foods[4]......................	0.444	0.9	0.004	0.70	S-Nov.2014	0.9
Prepared salads[6,5]..............................		3.4		1.20	S-Nov.2014	3.2
Food away from home..............................	5.830	3.1	0.175	0.17	L-Feb.2012	3.1
Full service meals and snacks[4]....................	2.823	3.0	0.083	0.23	S-Nov.2014	3.0
Limited service meals and snacks[4].................	2.413	3.4	0.080	0.29	L-Sep.2012	3.4
Food at employee sites and schools[4]...............	0.212	1.9	0.004	0.64	L-Nov.2014	2.1
Food at elementary and secondary schools[7,5].........		2.3		0.41	–	–
Food from vending machines and mobile vendors[4].......	0.064	1.7	0.001	1.22	L-Oct.2013	1.7
Other food away from home[4]..........................	0.319	2.2	0.007	0.44	L-Oct.2014	2.3
Energy................................	8.030	-19.6	-1.803	0.17	S-Sep.2009	-21.6
Energy commodities.................................	4.215	-34.7	-1.874	0.19	S-Jul.2009	-37.9
Fuel oil and other fuels.............................	0.236	-24.9	-0.073	0.81	S-Sep.2009	-32.2
Fuel oil...	0.139	-29.7	-0.053	0.82	S-Sep.2009	-36.0
Propane, kerosene, and firewood[8].................	0.097	-17.4	-0.020	1.48	S-Oct.2009	-17.4
Motor fuel..	3.979	-35.2	-1.801	0.20	S-Jul.2009	-37.7
Gasoline (all types)................................	3.904	-35.4	-1.780	0.20	S-Jul.2009	-37.3
Gasoline, unleaded regular[5]........................		-36.2		0.46	S-Jul.2009	-37.7
Gasoline, unleaded midgrade[9,5].....................		-34.0		0.52	S-Jul.2009	-36.6
Gasoline, unleaded premium[5]........................		-31.3		0.38	S-Jul.2009	-35.5
Other motor fuels[4]..............................	0.075	-24.2	-0.021	0.26	S-Oct.2009	-28.3
Energy services[10].................................	3.815	1.9	0.071	0.30	S-Mar.2013	1.1
Electricity[10].....................................	2.940	2.5	0.074	0.38	S-Apr.2014	2.1
Utility (piped) gas service[10].......................	0.875	-0.4	-0.004	0.49	S-Jan.2013	-2.5
All items less food and energy........................	77.713	1.6	1.268	0.10	–	–
Commodities less food and energy commodities...........	19.408	-0.8	-0.156	0.24	–	–
Household furnishings and supplies[11].................	3.342	-2.1	-0.073	0.30	S-Sep.2014	-2.4
Window and floor coverings and other linens[4]..........	0.266	-4.0	-0.011	1.12	S-Nov.2013	-4.1
Floor coverings[4]..............................	0.047	1.3	0.001	1.00	L-Sep.2014	2.1
Window coverings[4].............................	0.053	-4.4	-0.002	1.32	S-Apr.2011	-4.9
Other linens[4].................................	0.166	-5.3	-0.010	1.68	S-Nov.2013	-5.4
Furniture and bedding..............................	0.769	-2.2	-0.017	0.70	S-Nov.2014	-2.2
Bedroom furniture...............................	0.268	-4.2	-0.012	1.13	S-Sep.2010	-5.0
Living room, kitchen, and dining room furniture[4].....	0.363	-1.5	-0.006	1.16	L-Jan.2014	-0.7
Other furniture[4]...............................	0.128	0.3	0.000	1.75	S-Oct.2014	-1.0
Infants' furniture[7,5]............................						
Appliances[4].......................................	0.271	-4.9	-0.014	0.92	L-Nov.2014	-4.9
Major appliances[4]..............................	0.147	-7.7	-0.012	1.24	S-Nov.2014	-7.7
Laundry equipment[5].............................		-8.4		1.34	S-Nov.2014	-10.2
Other appliances[4]..............................	0.120	-1.3	-0.002	1.22	L-Nov.2014	-1.3
Other household equipment and furnishings[4]...........	0.479	-3.3	-0.016	0.97	L-Oct.2014	-2.7
Clocks, lamps, and decorator items..................	0.257	-4.3	-0.012	1.78	L-Oct.2014	-3.9
Indoor plants and flowers[12].......................	0.107	1.6	0.002	1.42	S-Nov.2014	1.1
Dishes and flatware[4].............................	0.041	-6.6	-0.003	2.60	L-Nov.2014	-5.2
Nonelectric cookware and tableware[4].................	0.074	-4.1	-0.003	1.20	S-Aug.2014	-5.5

See footnotes at end of table.

Table 7. Consumer Price Index for All Urban Consumers (CPI-U): U.S. city average, by expenditure category, January 2015, 12-month analysis table — Continued
[1982-84=100, unless otherwise noted]

Expenditure category	Relative importance Dec. 2014	Twelve Month				
		Unadjusted percent change Jan. 2014-Jan. 2015	Unadjusted effect on All Items Jan. 2014-Jan. 2015[1]	Standard error, median price change[2]	Largest (L) or Smallest (S) unadjusted change since:[3]	
					Date	Percent change
Tools, hardware, outdoor equipment and supplies[4]....	0.710	-0.6	-0.004	0.69	S-Sep.2014	-1.7
Tools, hardware and supplies[4].........................	0.189	0.8	0.001	1.14	–	–
Outdoor equipment and supplies[4].....................	0.367	-1.3	-0.005	0.82	S-Sep.2014	-2.3
Housekeeping supplies.....................................	0.847	-1.1	-0.010	0.45	S-Jun.2014	-1.1
Household cleaning products[4]..........................	0.337	-2.0	-0.007	0.73	S-Sep.2014	-2.2
Household paper products[4]............................	0.247	-1.1	-0.003	0.95	S-Dec.2003	-1.8
Miscellaneous household products[4]...................	0.263	-0.1	0.000	0.87	L-Nov.2014	-0.1
Apparel...	3.343	-1.4	-0.047	1.10	L-Nov.2014	-0.3
Men's and boys' apparel................................	0.834	-2.2	-0.019	1.58	L-Nov.2014	-1.7
Men's apparel...	0.653	-2.4	-0.016	1.68	L-Nov.2014	-1.2
Men's suits, sport coats, and outerwear...........	0.104	-5.4	-0.006	4.45	L-Nov.2014	-3.7
Men's furnishings......................................	0.185	-4.4	-0.008	1.95	S-Sep.2007	-4.5
Men's shirts and sweaters[4].........................	0.196	-5.4	-0.011	3.27	S-Aug.2014	-5.7
Men's pants and shorts................................	0.160	5.8	0.009	2.93	L-Oct.2013	6.6
Boys' apparel..	0.181	-1.2	-0.002	3.15	L-Jul.2014	2.8
Women's and girls' apparel.............................	1.439	-2.9	-0.042	2.28	L-Nov.2014	-0.4
Women's apparel.......................................	1.210	-3.5	-0.043	2.36	–	–
Women's outerwear....................................	0.118	6.2	0.007	6.49	L-Oct.2014	8.8
Women's dresses......................................	0.155	-2.1	-0.003	11.82	S-Jun.2013	-4.3
Women's suits and separates[4]......................	0.550	-7.7	-0.045	2.53	L-Nov.2014	-3.0
Women's underwear, nightwear, sportswear and accessories[4].....................................	0.378	-0.4	-0.002	2.23	S-Apr.2013	-0.4
Girls' apparel..	0.229	0.7	0.002	5.34	L-Oct.2014	1.3
Footwear...	0.725	2.6	0.018	1.58	S-Nov.2014	2.0
Men's footwear...	0.218	0.1	0.000	2.42	S-Apr.2014	0.0
Boys' and girls' footwear..............................	0.178	5.4	0.009	2.48	S-Jun.2014	3.9
Women's footwear.....................................	0.329	2.8	0.009	2.86	L-Aug.2013	3.0
Infants' and toddlers' apparel.........................	0.135	0.8	0.001	2.06	L-Nov.2014	1.1
Jewelry and watches[8]................................	0.211	-2.8	-0.006	1.91	L-Sep.2014	-2.3
Watches[8]...	0.046	2.3	0.001	2.38	L-Oct.2014	2.6
Jewelry[8]..	0.164	-4.1	-0.007	2.38	L-Sep.2014	-3.8
Transportation commodities less motor fuel[11]...........	5.685	-0.9	-0.051	0.23	–	–
New vehicles...	3.551	0.5	0.016	0.34	–	–
New cars and trucks[4, 5].............................		0.5		0.32	S-Sep.2014	0.3
New cars[5]..		-0.2		0.35	S-Sep.2014	-0.4
New trucks[13, 5]......................................		1.1		0.35	S-Sep.2014	1.0
Used cars and trucks..................................	1.591	-4.0	-0.067	0.12	L-Nov.2014	-3.1
Motor vehicle parts and equipment...................	0.435	-0.4	-0.002	0.42	L-Mar.2013	-0.3
Tires...	0.285	-1.3	-0.004	0.58	L-Mar.2013	-1.3
Vehicle accessories other than tires[4]..............	0.150	1.5	0.002	0.51	S-Nov.2014	1.5
Vehicle parts and equipment other than tires[5]...		1.0		0.66	S-Nov.2014	1.0
Motor oil, coolant, and fluids[5]......................		2.4		0.81	–	–
Medical care commodities.................................	1.772	3.9	0.067	0.64	S-Nov.2014	3.1
Medicinal drugs[11].....................................	1.696	4.2	0.068	0.66	S-Nov.2014	3.3
Prescription drugs.....................................	1.345	5.6	0.072	0.82	S-Nov.2014	4.6
Nonprescription drugs[11]..............................	0.351	-1.1	-0.004	0.81	S-Nov.2014	-1.4
Medical equipment and supplies[11].....................	0.076	-1.0	-0.001	1.18	S-Jun.2014	-1.1
Recreation commodities[11]................................	2.007	-2.8	-0.058	0.45	S-Nov.2014	-2.8
Video and audio products[11]............................	0.289	-10.3	-0.033	0.71	L-Nov.2014	-10.0
Televisions...	0.133	-16.7	-0.027	1.27	–	–
Other video equipment[4].............................	0.029	1.2	0.000	2.04	L-Oct.2014	4.6
Audio equipment......................................	0.066	-7.9	-0.006	1.54	S-Nov.2014	-8.1
Audio discs, tapes and other media[4]................	0.044	-2.8	-0.001	1.31	L-Sep.2014	-2.4
Pets and pet products...................................	0.659	-0.3	-0.002	0.75	S-Nov.2014	-0.5

See footnotes at end of table.

Expenditure category	Relative importance Dec. 2014	Twelve Month				
		Unadjusted percent change Jan. 2014-Jan. 2015	Unadjusted effect on All Items Jan. 2014-Jan. 2015[1]	Standard error, median price change[2]	Largest (L) or Smallest (S) unadjusted change since:[3]	
					Date	Percent change
Pet food[4, 5]		-0.4		0.73	S-Aug.2014	-0.5
Purchase of pets, pet supplies, accessories[4, 5]		0.1		1.57	S-Nov.2014	-0.5
Sporting goods	0.400	-1.9	-0.008	0.98	L-Oct.2014	-0.8
Sports vehicles including bicycles	0.181	-0.8	-0.002	1.25	L-Oct.2014	0.2
Sports equipment	0.214	-2.8	-0.006	1.25	L-Oct.2014	-1.8
Photographic equipment and supplies	0.058	-4.3	-0.003	2.13	S-Mar.2014	-6.4
Film and photographic supplies[4, 5]		14.7		3.72	S-Jan.2014	12.7
Photographic equipment[4, 5]		-7.3		2.32	S-Mar.2014	-10.4
Recreational reading materials	0.220	2.1	0.005	1.23	S-Nov.2014	1.9
Newspapers and magazines[4]	0.123	4.6	0.005	1.55	S-Nov.2014	3.8
Recreational books[4]	0.094	-0.9	-0.001	1.76	–	–
Other recreational goods[4]	0.381	-4.2	-0.017	1.31	S-Nov.2014	-4.7
Toys	0.277	-5.3	-0.016	1.52	L-Feb.2014	-5.1
Toys, games, hobbies and playground equipment[4, 5]		-2.4		1.31	L-Dec.2013	-2.2
Sewing machines, fabric and supplies[4]	0.050	-2.6	-0.001	3.78	S-Dec.2013	-4.4
Music instruments and accessories[4]	0.042	1.1	0.000	1.24	S-Oct.2014	1.1
Education and communication commodities[11]	0.610	-4.4	-0.028	0.87	L-Nov.2014	-4.0
Educational books and supplies	0.203	6.5	0.013	1.22	L-May 2013	6.7
College textbooks[14, 5]		7.4		1.32	L-Jun.2013	7.4
Information technology commodities[11]	0.408	-9.1	-0.041	1.09	S-Apr.2012	-9.6
Personal computers and peripheral equipment[6]	0.272	-10.4	-0.032	1.27	L-Nov.2014	-8.0
Computer software and accessories[4]	0.068	-1.8	-0.001	1.91	S-Oct.2014	-3.5
Telephone hardware, calculators, and other consumer information items[4]	0.068	-10.6	-0.008	3.25	S-Nov.2014	-10.6
Alcoholic beverages	1.015	1.0	0.010	0.31	S-Jul.2014	0.6
Alcoholic beverages at home	0.597	0.1	0.001	0.46	S-Jul.2014	-0.1
Beer, ale, and other malt beverages at home	0.274	0.2	0.000	0.51	S-Dec.2005	-0.5
Distilled spirits at home	0.073	0.5	0.000	0.63	S-Aug.2014	0.5
Whiskey at home[5]		2.0		1.12	L-Jul.2014	2.3
Distilled spirits, excluding whiskey, at home[5]		0.1		1.00	S-Oct.2014	0.1
Wine at home	0.250	-0.1	0.000	0.86	S-Sep.2014	-0.2
Alcoholic beverages away from home	0.418	2.3	0.010	0.42	L-Dec.2013	2.3
Beer, ale, and other malt beverages away from home[4, 5]		1.8		0.55	S-Oct.2014	1.8
Wine away from home[4, 5]		2.4		0.80	L-Dec.2013	2.4
Distilled spirits away from home[4, 5]		2.6		0.61	L-Dec.2013	2.7
Other goods[11]	1.634	1.5	0.025	0.40	L-Nov.2014	1.5
Tobacco and smoking products	0.718	2.4	0.017	0.44	S-Sep.2014	2.0
Cigarettes[4]	0.661	2.5	0.016	0.46	S-Sep.2014	2.2
Tobacco products other than cigarettes[4]	0.050	0.6	0.000	1.26	S-Oct.2014	0.3
Personal care products	0.724	1.3	0.009	0.79	L-Oct.2014	1.7
Hair, dental, shaving, and miscellaneous personal care products[4]	0.369	0.5	0.002	1.10	L-Sep.2014	0.8
Cosmetics, perfume, bath, nail preparations and implements	0.348	2.1	0.007	1.18	L-Nov.2014	2.4
Miscellaneous personal goods[4]	0.192	-0.6	-0.001	1.06	–	–
Stationery, stationery supplies, gift wrap[5]		-0.8		1.13	S-Feb.2014	-1.2
Infants' equipment[7, 5]		-1.3		1.47	S-Nov.2014	-2.3
Services less energy services	58.305	2.5	1.424	0.11	L-Nov.2014	2.5
Shelter	32.711	2.9	0.940	0.16	–	–
Rent of shelter[15]	32.336	2.9	0.920	0.16	–	–
Rent of primary residence[10]	7.159	3.4	0.237	0.17	–	–
Lodging away from home[4]	0.839	6.6	0.055	2.00	L-Oct.2014	8.4

See footnotes at end of table.

Table 7. Consumer Price Index for All Urban Consumers (CPI-U): U.S. city average, by expenditure category, January 2015, 12-month analysis table — Continued

[1982-84=100, unless otherwise noted]

Expenditure category	Relative importance Dec. 2014	Twelve Month				
		Unadjusted percent change Jan. 2014- Jan. 2015	Unadjusted effect on All Items Jan. 2014- Jan. 2015[1]	Standard error, median price change[2]	Largest (L) or Smallest (S) unadjusted change since:[3]	
					Date	Percent change
Housing at school, excluding board[10, 15]..........	0.172	2.7	0.005	0.26	–	–
Other lodging away from home including hotels and motels....	0.666	7.6	0.050	2.41	L-Oct.2014	9.8
Owners' equivalent rent of residences[10, 15]...........	24.339	2.6	0.629	0.16	–	–
Owners' equivalent rent of primary residence[10, 15]...........	22.918	2.6	0.592	0.16	–	–
Tenants' and household insurance[4]....................	0.375	5.6	0.020	0.95	–	–
Water and sewer and trash collection services[4]........	1.222	4.5	0.053	0.47	S-Nov.2014	4.3
Water and sewerage maintenance[10]..................	0.945	5.5	0.050	0.55	S-Nov.2014	5.1
Garbage and trash collection[13].......................	0.277	1.3	0.003	0.61	S-May 1996	1.0
Household operations[4]....................................	0.848	3.0	0.025	0.38	L-Nov.2014	3.2
Domestic services[4].....................................	0.279	1.7	0.005	0.42	L-Nov.2014	2.0
Gardening and lawncare services[4].....................	0.279		0.011	0.58	–	–
Moving, storage, freight expense[4]......................	0.116	2.9	0.003	1.30	L-Oct.2014	3.7
Repair of household items[4]............................	0.066	4.4	0.003	0.70	L-Oct.2013	4.5
Medical care services....................................	5.944	2.3	0.133	0.24	S-Nov.2014	2.3
Professional services....................................	3.032	1.7	0.051	0.30	–	–
Physicians' services[10]............................	1.590	1.7	0.026	0.46	L-May 2014	1.7
Dental services[10].................................	0.804	2.2	0.017	0.54	L-May 2014	2.2
Eyeglasses and eye care[8]..........................	0.284	1.4	0.004	0.74	S-Oct.2014	1.4
Services by other medical professionals[10, 8].......	0.354	1.1	0.004	0.56	S-Sep.2014	0.7
Hospital and related services..........................	2.159	4.1	0.085	0.41	S-Oct.2014	3.9
Hospital services[10, 16]...............................	1.853	4.3	0.077	0.46	S-Oct.2014	4.2
Inpatient hospital services[10, 16, 5]................		4.3		0.91	S-Jul.2013	2.8
Outpatient hospital services[10, 8, 5]...............		4.4		0.63	S-Nov.2014	4.2
Nursing homes and adult day services[10, 16].......	0.174	3.4	0.006	0.44	L-Jan.2013	3.4
Care of invalids and elderly at home[7]..............	0.132	1.8	0.002	0.74	–	–
Health insurance[7]......................................	0.753	-0.5	-0.004	0.25	–	–
Transportation services..................................	5.625	2.1	0.117	0.31	L-Jun.2014	3.2
Leased cars and trucks[14].............................	0.397	0.8	0.003	1.26	L-Nov.2009	1.4
Car and truck rental[4]...................................	0.073	1.4	0.001	2.42	L-Nov.2014	4.1
Motor vehicle maintenance and repair.................	1.168	2.0	0.022	0.33	S-Oct.2014	1.9
Motor vehicle body work............................	0.057	1.9	0.001	0.68	S-Nov.2014	1.9
Motor vehicle maintenance and servicing..........	0.492	1.6	0.008	0.44	S-Sep.2014	1.5
Motor vehicle repair[4]..............................	0.587	2.3	0.013	0.53	L-Mar.2012	2.3
Motor vehicle insurance..............................	2.300	5.0	0.110	0.59	L-Feb.2013	5.2
Motor vehicle fees[4].....................................	0.565	0.1	0.001	0.45	S-Sep.2014	-0.3
State motor vehicle registration and license fees[10, 4].....	0.312	-1.2	-0.004	0.66	S-EVER	–
Parking and other fees[4].............................	0.235	1.7	0.004	0.47	S-Oct.2014	1.5
Parking fees and tolls[4, 5]...........................		2.3		0.63	S-Nov.2014	1.9
Automobile service clubs[4, 5].......................		-0.4		0.75	–	–
Public transportation.....................................	1.122	-1.8	-0.020	0.75	L-Oct.2014	-1.8
Airline fare...	0.702	-3.0	-0.021	0.98	L-Oct.2014	-2.8
Other intercity transportation.........................	0.157	-1.6	-0.002	1.86	S-Oct.2014	-2.1
Intercity bus fare[6, 5]...............................						
Intercity train fare[6, 5].............................		1.6		1.59	S-Oct.2014	0.2
Ship fare[4, 5]......................................		-1.1		2.34	L-Aug.2014	0.3
Intracity transportation................................	0.260	1.4	0.004	0.22	L-Feb.2014	3.4
Intracity mass transit[11, 5].........................		1.1		0.59	–	–
Recreation services[11]...................................	3.744	1.6	0.059	0.52	L-Aug.2014	1.7
Video and audio services[11]...........................	1.558	1.8	0.028	0.39	–	–
Cable and satellite television and radio service[13]...........	1.468	2.1	0.030	0.40	S-Nov.2014	1.8

See footnotes at end of table.

Table 7. Consumer Price Index for All Urban Consumers (CPI-U): U.S. city average, by expenditure category, January 2015, 12-month analysis table — Continued
[1982-84=100, unless otherwise noted]

Expenditure category	Relative importance Dec. 2014	Twelve Month				
		Unadjusted percent change Jan. 2014-Jan. 2015	Unadjusted effect on All Items Jan. 2014-Jan. 2015[1]	Standard error, median price change[2]	Largest (L) or Smallest (S) unadjusted change since:[3]	
					Date	Percent change
Video discs and other media, including rental of video and audio[4]	0.090	-2.6	-0.002	1.79	L-Sep.2013	-2.1
Video discs and other media[4, 5]		-6.3		2.46	–	–
Rental of video or audio discs and other media[4, 5]		2.5		0.99	L-Aug.2012	5.3
Pet services including veterinary[4]	0.399	2.9	0.012	0.44	L-Nov.2014	2.9
Pet services[4, 5]		1.8		1.08	–	–
Veterinarian services[4, 5]		3.2		0.58	L-Nov.2014	3.2
Photographers and film processing[4]	0.062	2.1	0.001	1.18	S-Nov.2014	2.0
Photographer fees[4, 5]		1.1		0.77	–	–
Film processing[4, 5]		4.0		1.23	L-Apr.2011	4.6
Other recreation services[4]	1.724	1.1	0.018	1.03	L-Aug.2014	1.6
Club dues and fees for participant sports and group exercises[4]	0.602	0.6	0.004	1.34	L-Aug.2014	2.0
Admissions	0.640	0.9	0.006	1.31	L-Oct.2014	1.2
Admission to movies, theaters, and concerts[4, 5]		0.2		0.98	S-Nov.2014	0.0
Admission to sporting events[4, 5]		3.6		1.47	L-Jul.2014	3.7
Fees for lessons or instructions[8]	0.211	2.0	0.004	0.60	–	–
Education and communication services[11]	6.452	0.9	0.059	0.19	–	–
Tuition, other school fees, and childcare	3.122	3.5	0.107	0.31	L-Jun.2014	3.6
College tuition and fees	1.853	3.6	0.066	0.45	L-Jul.2014	3.9
Elementary and high school tuition and fees	0.377	4.0	0.014	0.42	–	–
Child care and nursery school[12]	0.725	3.0	0.022	0.52	L-Oct.2011	3.1
Technical and business school tuition and fees[4]	0.039	2.0	0.001	0.48	L-Aug.2014	2.0
Postage and delivery services[4]	0.144	3.4	0.005	0.35	S-Jan.2012	1.3
Postage	0.130	3.6	0.005	0.38	S-Jan.2012	0.8
Delivery services[4]	0.014	1.9	0.000	0.53	L-Oct.2014	3.2
Telephone services[4]	2.462	-2.5	-0.065	0.30	S-Dec.2004	-2.5
Wireless telephone services[4]	1.624	-4.3	-0.074	0.39	S-Dec.2001	-5.5
Land-line telephone services[11]	0.837	1.1	0.009	0.42	S-EVER	–
Internet services and electronic information providers[4]	0.711	1.8	0.013	0.75	L-Nov.2014	1.8
Other personal services[11]	1.760	2.1	0.037	0.29	L-Dec.2013	2.1
Personal care services	0.638	1.4	0.009	0.43	S-Nov.2014	1.3
Haircuts and other personal care services[4]	0.638	1.4	0.009	0.43	S-Nov.2014	1.3
Miscellaneous personal services	1.122	2.5	0.028	0.40	L-Jun.2013	2.5
Legal services[8]	0.316	1.2	0.004	0.66	S-Mar.1993	1.0
Funeral expenses[8]	0.173	1.4	0.002	0.63	L-Nov.2014	1.6
Laundry and dry cleaning services[4]	0.276	2.2	0.006	0.42	–	–
Apparel services other than laundry and dry cleaning[4]	0.034	2.0	0.001	0.68	L-Nov.2014	2.3
Financial services[8]	0.228	5.7	0.013	1.01	L-Sep.2012	6.0
Checking account and other bank services[4, 5]		0.1		0.60	–	–
Tax return preparation and other accounting fees[4, 5]		9.3		1.40	L-EVER	–
Special aggregate indexes						
All items less food	85.743	-0.6	-0.535	0.09	S-Sep.2009	-1.5
All items less shelter	67.289	-1.5	-1.030	0.10	S-Sep.2009	-2.2
All items less food and shelter	53.032	-2.7	-1.476	0.12	S-Sep.2009	-2.7
All items less food, shelter, and energy	45.002	0.7	0.328	0.13	–	–
All items less food, shelter, energy, and used cars and trucks	43.411	0.9	0.394	0.14	–	–
All items less medical care	92.284	-0.3	-0.289	0.08	S-Oct.2009	-0.4

See footnotes at end of table.

Table 7. Consumer Price Index for All Urban Consumers (CPI-U): U.S. city average, by expenditure category, January 2015, 12-month analysis table — Continued

[1982-84=100, unless otherwise noted]

Expenditure category	Relative importance Dec. 2014	Twelve Month				
		Unadjusted percent change Jan. 2014- Jan. 2015	Unadjusted effect on All Items Jan. 2014- Jan. 2015[1]	Standard error, median price change[2]	Largest (L) or Smallest (S) unadjusted change since:[3]	
					Date	Percent change
All items less energy...	91.970	1.9	1.714	0.08	–	–
Commodities..	37.880	-4.1	-1.584	0.13	S-Sep.2009	-4.2
Commodities less food, energy, and used cars and trucks..	17.817	-0.5	-0.089	0.27	–	–
Commodities less food....................................	23.623	-8.1	-2.030	0.19	S-Jul.2009	-9.2
Commodities less food and beverages................	22.608	-8.5	-2.040	0.20	S-Jul.2009	-9.6
Services...	62.120	2.4	1.494	0.10	S-Feb.2014	2.4
Services less rent of shelter[15]............................	29.784	1.9	0.574	0.12	S-Sep.2012	1.9
Services less medical care services.....................	56.176	2.5	1.361	0.11	–	–
Durables...	8.950	-2.0	-0.184	0.19	–	–
Nondurables..	28.930	-4.7	-1.399	0.16	S-Sep.2009	-5.4
Nondurables less food.....................................	14.673	-11.6	-1.845	0.26	S-Jul.2009	-13.8
Nondurables less food and beverages.................	13.658	-12.5	-1.856	0.28	S-Jul.2009	-14.8
Nondurables less food, beverages, and apparel...........	10.315	-15.8	-1.808	0.17	S-Jul.2009	-18.9
Nondurables less food and apparel......................	11.330	-14.4	-1.798	0.15	S-Jul.2009	-17.3
Housing..	42.173	2.3	0.943	0.13	S-Dec.2013	2.2
Education and communication[4]................................	7.062	0.4	0.031	0.20	–	–
Education[4]...	3.325	3.7	0.119	0.30	L-Jul.2013	3.8
Communication[4]...	3.737	-2.3	-0.089	0.25	S-Aug.2005	-2.4
Information and information processing[4]...................	3.593	-2.5	-0.093	0.26	S-Aug.2005	-2.6
Information technology, hardware and services[17]........	1.132	-2.5	-0.029	0.66	–	–
Recreation[4]..	5.750	0.0	0.001	0.35	–	–
Video and audio[4]..	1.847	-0.3	-0.006	0.36	–	–
Pets, pet products and services[4]............................	1.058	0.9	0.010	0.48	S-Nov.2014	0.8
Photography[4]..	0.120	-1.0	-0.001	1.30	S-Mar.2014	-1.8
Food and beverages...	15.272	3.1	0.456	0.12	S-Nov.2014	3.1
Domestically produced farm food...........................	7.094	3.7	0.257	0.20	S-Nov.2014	3.7
Other services..	11.955	1.3	0.155	0.20	L-Oct.2014	1.4
Apparel less footwear...	2.619	-2.4	-0.065	1.32	L-Nov.2014	-0.9
Fuels and utilities..	5.273	1.0	0.051	0.23	S-Jan.2013	0.9
Household energy...	4.051	-0.1	-0.003	0.29	S-Jan.2013	-0.4
Medical care..	7.716	2.6	0.200	0.24	S-Nov.2014	2.5
Transportation..	15.289	-10.6	-1.735	0.16	S-Aug.2009	-10.8
Private transportation.......................................	14.167	-11.2	-1.714	0.16	S-Jul.2009	-14.3
New and used motor vehicles[4]...........................	5.720	-0.8	-0.045	0.25	L-Nov.2014	-0.7
Utilities and public transportation..............................	10.089	0.7	0.069	0.17	S-Oct.2012	0.2
Household furnishings and operations........................	4.109	-1.1	-0.048	0.25	S-Sep.2014	-1.4
Other goods and services.....................................	3.394	1.8	0.062	0.25	L-Oct.2014	1.9
Personal care..	2.676	1.7	0.045	0.31	L-Oct.2014	1.7

[1] The 'effect' of an item category is a measure of that item's contribution to the All items price change. For example, if the Food index had an effect of 0.40, and the All items index rose 1.2 percent, then the increase in food prices contributed 0.40 / 1.2, or 33.3 percent, to that All items increase. Said another way, had food prices been unchanged for that year the change in the All items index would have been 1.2 percent minus 0.40, or 0.8 percent. Effects can be negative as well. For example, if the effect of food was a negative 0.1, and the All items index rose 0.5 percent, the All items index actually would have been 0.1 percent higher (or 0.6 percent) had food prices been unchanged. Since food prices fell while prices overall were rising, the contribution of food to the All items price change was negative (in this case, -0.1 / 0.5, or minus 20 percent).

[2] A statistic's margin of error is often expressed as its point estimate plus or minus two standard errors. For example, if a CPI category rose 2.6 percent, and its standard error was 0.25 percent, the margin of error on this item's 12-month percent change would be 2.6 percent, plus or minus 0.5 percent.

[3] If the current 12-month percent change is greater than the previous published 12-month percent change, then this column identifies the closest prior month with a 12-month percent change as (L)arge as or (L)arger than the current 12-month change. If the current 12-month percent change is smaller than the previous published 12-month percent change, the most recent month with a change as (S)mall or (S)maller than the current month change is identified. If the current and previous published 12-month percent changes are equal, a dash will appear. Standard numerical comparison is used. For example, 2.0% is greater than 0.6%, -4.4% is less than -2.0%, and -2.0% is less than 0.0%. Note that a (L)arger change can be a smaller decline, for example, a -0.2% change is larger than a -0.4% change, but still represents a decline in the price index. Likewise, (S)maller changes can be increases, for example, a 0.6% change is smaller than 0.8%, but still represents an increase in the price index. In this context, a -0.2% change is considered to be smaller than a 0.0% change.

[4] Indexes on a December 1997=100 base.

[5] Special indexes based on a substantially smaller sample. These series do not contribute to the all items index aggregation and therefore do not have a relative importance or effect.

[6] Indexes on a December 2007=100 base.

[7] Indexes on a December 2005=100 base.

[8] Indexes on a December 1986=100 base.

[9] Indexes on a December 1993=100 base.

[10] This index series was calculated using a Laspeyres estimator. All other item stratum index series were calculated using a geometric means estimator.

[11] Indexes on a December 2009=100 base.

[12] Indexes on a December 1990=100 base.

[13] Indexes on a December 1983=100 base.

[14] Indexes on a December 2001=100 base.

[15] Indexes on a December 1982=100 base.

[16] Indexes on a December 1996=100 base.

[17] Indexes on a December 1988=100 base.

NOTE: Index applies to a month as a whole, not to any specific date.